De cabo a rabo

*The Most Comprehensive Guide to Learning
Spanish Ever Written*

Gramática

David Faulkner

**Flashforward
Publishing**

De cabo a rabo: Gramática

The Most Comprehensive Guide to Learning Spanish Ever Written

Published by Flashforward Publishing

Boulder, CO

Library of Congress Control Number: 2017937225

ISBN: 978-0-9964497-4-8 (softcover)
ISBN: 978-0-9964497-6-2 (hardcover)

FOREIGN LANGUAGE STUDY / Spanish

QUANTITY PURCHASES: Schools, companies, professional groups, clubs, and other organizations may qualify for special terms when ordering quantities of this title.
For information, please contact the author through DavidFaulknerBooks.com.

Flashforward
Publishing

Querid@ estudiante,

Whether you only know a few grammatical concepts in Spanish, or have been studying it for years, if you're looking to improve your understanding of Spanish grammar, you've come to the right place. I've broken *Gramática* down into 30 manageable units, which go hand in hand with *Vocabulario* and *Actividades*, to take you from the basics to advanced concepts and beyond.

My goal has been to create the most original, most user-friendly, and most comprehensive Spanish-learning guides in the world, leaving behind all the fluff typically found in your average language book. These guides are my life-long obsession with the Spanish language, on paper, accessible to all who want to improve and polish their Spanish language skills.

I have drawn on my personal experiences traveling and living in several Spanish-speaking countries on three continents. I have also drawn on my experiences in the classroom studying under professors from just about every Spanish-speaking country in the world. I have pushed my limits of linguistic understanding (as well as theirs) in an attempt to understand every aspect, subtlety, and nuance of the language. I've tried to make these guides multi-regional—if not universal—in order to give you the greatest chance of communicating effectively with any native Spanish speaker in the world. Despite their intended universality, they cannot train your ear nor can they give you feedback. In addition to *Gramática*, *Vocabulario*, and *Actividades*, to truly master the language, you will need as much authentic audio input as you can get your ears on: movies, music, TV, friends, neighbors, and strangers. The world is your classroom! Working with an experienced teacher (or ten, over the years) to give you precise feedback will also facilitate your language acquisition.

Whatever your motivation to improve your Spanish may be, I hope these guides continue to serve you well for many years to come. Mastering a new language is one of the most difficult things you could ever attempt and it requires persistence, humility, and patience. Don't be discouraged if understanding certain concepts escapes you the first, second, or even third time around. Every time you come back and review them, with new experiences under your belt, you will see them with new eyes and, one day, they'll finally click. "When the student is ready, the teacher will appear," and every time you re-read one of these units, even though the wording hasn't changed, you will likely learn something you hadn't previously picked up on. With that, I wish you great success!

Un abrazo,

David

Contenido

Unidad 1 – cognates, prefixes and suffixes, pronunciation and emphasis   5

Unidad 2 – gender and number, *ser*, *estar*, *gustar*, indirect-object pronouns, questions   7

Unidad 3 – present tense (regular verbs), possessive adjectives   12

Unidad 4 – present tense (irregular verbs), infinitives and compound verb structures   14

Unidad 5 – idiomatic expressions with *tener*   17

Unidad 6 – adjectives, adverbs, comparatives   18

Unidad 7 – direct-object pronouns, questions   19

Unidad 8 – progressive present, gerund and infinitives   20

Unidad 9 – present tense (irregulars), *hay*, *tener*, direct-object pronouns   21

Unidad 10 – *ser*, *estar*, indirect-object pronouns, *doler*, double negatives, reflexive verbs   23

Unidad 11 – preterite tense (regulars and irregulars)   28

Unidad 12 – present tense (irregulars), *conocer*, *saber*, preterite tense (irregulars)   31

Unidad 13 – reflexive present-tense verbs, reflexive preterite-tense verbs   36

Unidad 14 – direct objects with reflexive verbs, comparatives, nominalization of adjectives   39

Unidad 15 – indirect-object pronouns with direct-object pronouns   42

Unidad 16 – present tense (irregulars), preterite tense (irregulars), gerund forms (irregulars)   44

Unidad 17 – imperfect tense (regulars and irregulars)   48

Unidad 18 – accent marks, combining object pronouns (R.I.D.), "personal a"   50

Unidad 19 – progressive tenses, *tú* commands (regulars and irregulars, reflexive)   54

Unidad 20 – *tú*/*Ud.*/*Uds.* commands, accent marks, comparatives, superlatives   57

Unidad 21 – past participles as adjectives and present-perfect tense (regulars and irregulars)   62

Unidad 22 – pluperfect tense (regulars and irregulars)   66

Unidad 23 – future tense (regulars and irregulars), future-perfect tense, subjunctive mood   67

Unidad 24 – present subjunctive (regulars and irregulars), present-perfect subjunctive   71

Unidad 25 – subjunctive mood or indicative mood, routine or future   76

Unidad 26 – subjunctive mood, preterite or imperfect indicative   79

Unidad 27 – conditional tense, imperfect subjunctive (regulars and irregulars), infinitives   81

Unidad 28 – hypothetical situations, conditional-perfect, pluperfect subjunctive   84

Unidad 29 – gender and number, adjective placement, adverbs, diminutives, *ser*, *estar*, *haber*   88

Unidad 30 – accentuation and intonation, pronunciation, alphabet, spelling oddities   98

Unidad X – *se*, speculation, *vosotros*, *voseo*, prepositions, *por*, *para*, poorly spoken Spanish   105

Unidad 1

Los cognados – Cognates

Definition: related by descent from the same ancestral language – Merriam Webster Collegiate Dictionary. 10th Edition

Identifying *cognates* is one way to effortlessly increase your vocabulary in Spanish.

> *Ej.* calendario, computadora, secretario, actividad, alfabeto, falso, foto, teléfono, etc.

¡Ojo! – Watch out for false cognates!

> *Ej. embarazada* – pregnant, *actual* – current, *librería* – book store, etc.

Los prefijos y sufijos – Prefixes and Suffixes

Identifying *prefixes* is another great way to effortlessly increase your understanding of a word.

> *Ej.* bendición – blessing (good), maldición – curse (bad)

Identifying *suffixes* can help you understand the parts of speech of thousands of cognates.

> *Ej.* ción – tion (acción – action, celebración – celebration, condición – condition)
>
> dad – ty (universidad – university, habilidad – ability, posibilidad – possibility)
>
> sía – sy (cortesía – courtesy, fantasía – fantasy)
>
> tura – ture (aventura – adventure, cultura – culture)

Las frases y palabras útiles – Useful Words and Phrases

- **La gramática – Grammar**

  el adjetivo – adjective

  el adverbio – adverb

  el artículo definido – definite article

  > *el, la, los, las – the*

  el artículo indefinido – indefinite article

  > *un, una – a(n)*
  >
  > *unos, unas – some*

  concordar / la concordancia – to agree / agreement

  el complemento (in)directo – (in)direct object

  el pronombre – pronoun

  el sustantivo / el nombre – noun

  el verbo – verb

  el género - gender

  > masculino – masculine
  >
  > femenino – feminine

  el número - number

  > plural – plural
  >
  > singular – singular

  ¿ – used to open a question

  ¡ – used to open an exclamation

  por ejemplo (ej.) – for example (e.g.)

La pronunciación – Pronunciation

The subtleties of Spanish pronunciation can only be learned with a finely tuned ear and deliberate, focused practice to break your tongue of its habits. Here are some rough basics to help you in the beginning.

	Examples in English	Ejemplos en español
a	(f<u>a</u>ther)	(<u>a</u>gu<u>a</u>)
e	(m<u>e</u>t)	(<u>e</u>r<u>e</u>s)
i	(b<u>ee</u>)	(m<u>i</u>)
o	(h<u>o</u>pe)	(h<u>o</u>la)
u	(l<u>oo</u>p)	(t<u>ú</u>)
<u>ce</u>/<u>ci</u>	(s) / (<u>th</u>anks – Castilian)	(cator<u>ce</u>, die<u>ci</u>ocho)
<u>ca</u>/<u>co</u>/<u>cu</u>	(k)	(<u>ca</u>torce, <u>có</u>mo, <u>cu</u>atro)
<u>ge</u>/<u>gi</u>	(h)	(<u>ge</u>neral, <u>gi</u>gante)
<u>ga</u>/<u>go</u>/gu	(go)	(<u>ga</u>raje, <u>go</u>bierno, <u>gu</u>ante)
h	silent (an <u>h</u>erb)	(<u>h</u>ola)
j	(<u>h</u>appy)	(<u>J</u>osé)
ll, y	(<u>y</u>awn)	(<u>y</u>o me <u>ll</u>amo)
ñ	(can<u>y</u>on)	(espa<u>ñ</u>ol)
qu	(k)	(<u>qu</u>é, <u>qu</u>iero)
rr	(p<u>rrrrrrrrrr</u>)	(co<u>rr</u>er)
y ("*i griega*")	(ee)	(<u>y</u> tú)
z	(s) / (<u>th</u>anks – Castilian)	(<u>z</u>apato)

¡Ojo! There are 27 letters in Spanish: the 26 English letters and *ñ* (k, l, m, n, <u>ñ</u>, o, p, q, r, s).

El énfasis – Emphasis

➢ If a word ends in a vowel, *n* or *s*, the emphasis falls on the second to the last syllable.

➢ If a word ends in any other letter, the emphasis falls on the last syllable.

A written accent mark has three purposes (none of which changes the sound of the vowel):

➢ to mark a deviation from the above two rules.

    Ej. están, típica, cómodo

➢ to distinguish it from other single-syllable words.

    Ej. sé / se – I know / herself, himself or themselves
         tú / tu – you / your
         sí / si – yes / if
         él / el – he / the
         qué / que – what / that

➢ to signal a question word.

    Ej. qué / lo que – what? / what   dónde / donde – where? / where
         cómo / como – how? / as, like   quién / quien – who? / who(m)
         cuál / lo cual – which? / which   por qué – why?
         cuándo / cuando – when? / when   cuánto – how much

Unidad 2

El género – Gender

- ### Los sustantivos – Nouns

All nouns, whether they are animate or inanimate objects, have gender. The gender of a noun referring to a person depends on the sex of the person: masculine for a man/boy, feminine for a woman/girl (with the exception of generic nouns like *person, family, people, victim*, etc.). The gender of a noun that refers to an object other than a person is independent of the noun's characteristics. For example, *la mesa – table*, is feminine, but not because it has feminine characteristics. Many masculine nouns end in *o* and many feminine nouns end in *a*.
> *Ej.* la computadora – computer, el carro – car

Many nouns, however, end in consonants or vowels other than *o* or *a*.
> *Ej.* la pared – wall, el reloj – clock/watch, el coche – car

Definite articles (*el, la, los, las* – the) are used more frequently in Spanish than in English, and with the gender of the noun playing a determining factor in which article is used, nouns should be learned with their corresponding definite article (*el* libro, *la* televisión). By learning the definite article along with the noun, the gender of the noun is easier to identify.
> *Ej. la* – feminine, *el* – masculine

There are a few examples where the article doesn't seem to match the noun, but if you know the correct article, you'll generally know the noun's gender.
> *Ej.* la radio, el mapa, el programa, la foto

- ### Los adjetivos – Adjectives

Adjectives, like nouns, have gender. Adjectives must always agree in gender with the nouns that they modify (note the article). If the noun is masculine, then the adjective is masculine, etc. If the adjective does not end in *o* or *a* then it can modify both masculine and feminine nouns. Notice that, in Spanish, the adjective usually follows the noun it describes, unlike in English.
> *Ej.* el hombre <u>alto</u> – the <u>tall</u> man, la mujer <u>bonita</u> – the <u>beautiful</u> woman
> la silla <u>azul</u> – the <u>blue</u> chair, el carro <u>azul</u> – the <u>blue</u> car
> la foto <u>magnífica</u> – the <u>magnificent</u> photo, la pared <u>blanca</u> – the <u>white</u> wall

El número – Number

Adjectives must also agree in number with the nouns they modify: singular or plural.
> *Ej.* el profesor inteligente (singular), los profesores inteligentes (plural)

To make a noun or an adjective plural, follow these rules. Notice that *el* becomes *los*.
> ➢ If it ends in a vowel, add *s*.
> > *Ej.* el estudiante listo → lo<u>s</u> estudiante<u>s</u> listo<u>s</u>
> ➢ If it ends in a consonant, add *es*.
> > *Ej.* la pared blanca → la<u>s</u> pared<u>es</u> blanca<u>s</u>

Los verbos (el presente) – Verbs (present tense)

In English, we rarely have to think about how to conjugate verbs. In fact, if you have never studied a language other than English, you may not even know (by name) what conjugating a verb is. In order to explain verb conjugation, we must first know what an infinitive is. According to Webster, an infinitive is a verb form having the characteristics of both verb and noun. In English, it is usually used with the word *to*: *to walk*, *to swim*, etc. According to yours truly, it is the most basic and root form of a verb. To conjugate a verb is to change the infinitive so that the resulting form agrees with the subject.

> *Ej.* I walk. You walk. She walks. I swim. You swim. She swims.

In Spanish, each subject (1st person, singular; 1st person, plural; 2nd person, singular; 2nd person, plural; 3rd person, singular; and 3rd person, plural), in most tenses, has a unique verb conjugation. This is best illustrated with the following charts.

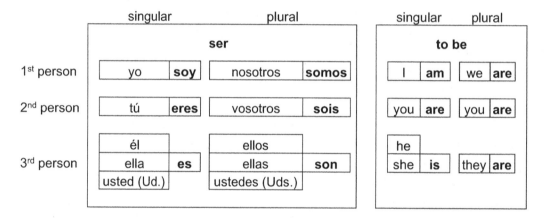

¡Ojo! Usted and *ustedes* are 2nd person, formal, but they are conjugated as 3rd person.

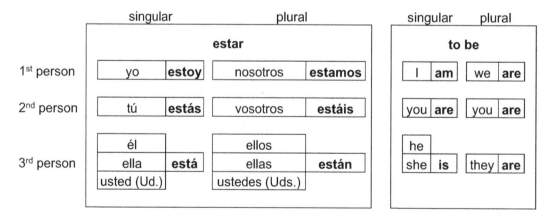

¡Ojo! The *vosotros* form is used primarily in Spain. In Latin America, *ustedes* serves as both the familiar and formal forms of *you, plural*.

8

Ser vs. estar

The verbs *ser* and *estar* both mean "to be." They each have specific uses and are not interchangeable. You have already seen both of these verbs in context.

> *Ej. ¿De dónde **eres**? **Soy** de Colorado.*
> *¿Cómo **estás**? **Estoy** bien, gracias.*

Take a look at some of the uses of each of these verbs.

- **Use *ser*:**

  - to describe origin. (<u>Soy</u> de Nevada.)

  - to describe time, days, dates, etc. (<u>Son</u> las 8:00 de la mañana.)

  - to describe physical characteristics. (El carro <u>es</u> verde. – The car is green.)

  - to describe character traits. (Eduardo <u>es</u> inteligente.)

- **Use *estar*:**

  - to describe location. (<u>Estamos</u> en Colorado. – We are in Colorado.)

  - to describe mental and emotional states. (<u>Estoy</u> triste. – I am sad.)

  - to describe physical states of being. (La comida <u>está</u> caliente. – The food is hot.)

Both *ser* and *estar* are used with adjectives to describe people and objects but they each have their distinct uses; they are not interchangeable.

Notice that the adjectives agree in both gender and number with the nouns they modify.

> *Ej.* Somos aburridos. – We are boring. (character trait)
> Estamos aburridos. – We are bored. (mental state)
>
> Soy listo. – I am clever/witty. (character trait)
> Estoy listo. – I am ready. (mental state)
>
> Soy preparada. – I am educated. (character trait)
> Estoy preparada. – I am prepared. (mental/physical state)
>
> Eres bonita. – You are pretty. (character trait)
> Estás bonita. – You look pretty. (physical state)
>
> Ellas son alegres. – They are happy people. (character trait)
> Ellas están alegres. – They are feeling happy. (mental state)
>
> El café es caliente. – Coffee is a hot drink. (physical characteristic)
> El café está frío. – The coffee is cold. (physical state)

Los verbos (el presente) – Verbs (present tense)

The following verbs, *gustar* and *encantar*, are most commonly used to express what a person *likes* or *loves*, respectively. Literally translated: what *pleases* that person or what *delights* that person. Therefore, they are not commonly conjugated like the verbs that we have already seen nor will see in the future. In Spanish, liking something is not active, but rather it is passive. Think of a food that you like or don't like. Do you have control over whether you like it or not? Can you simply change your mind about it? Take a look at the following comparisons.

In English, the subject does the liking and the thing being liked is the object.
Ej. **I** like chocolate. (how it is commonly said in English)

In Spanish, the subject does the pleasing and the object is the person that it pleases.
Ej. Chocolate pleases **me**. (literal translation from Spanish)

Notice that in the following constructions, the subject (what is doing the pleasing) is always in the 3rd person. The only difference is whether the thing doing the pleasing is singular or plural. The person receiving the pleasure of this/these thing(s) is the object and is represented by the corresponding indirect-object pronoun.

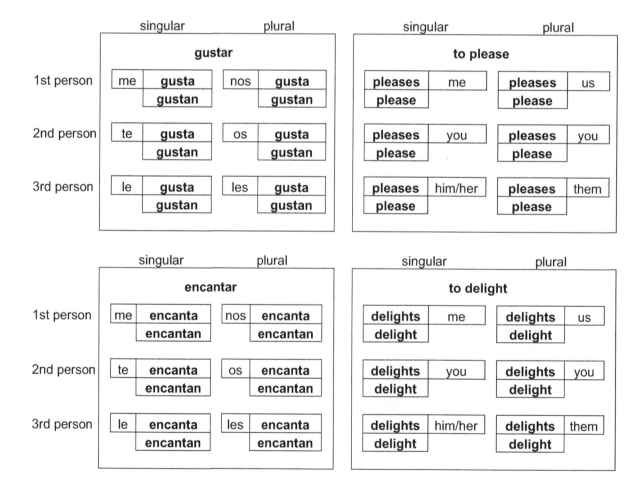

Los pronombres de complemento indirecto – Indirect-Object Pronouns

me – me	**nos** – us
te – you	**os** – you (Spain plural)
le – him / her / you (formal)	**les** – them / you (Latin America plural, formal)

Ej. (A mí) *me* gustan los coches. – I like cars. (Cars are pleasing to me.)

¿(A ti) *te* gusta cantar? – Do you like to sing? (Is singing pleasing to you?)

(A Pedro) <u>no</u> *le* encanta estudiar. – Pedro <u>doesn't</u> love to study.

(A mí y a María) *nos* encantan las flores. – We love flowers.

¿(A ti y a tus amigos) *os* gusta bailar? – Do you (all) like to dance?

(A Pedro y a María) *les* gusta leer. – Pedro and Maria like to read.

Regardless of the object of pleasure/delight, the subject in these examples is 3rd person, and is either singular or plural. Either "it pleases" or "they please." It would sound silly to say "it please" or "they pleases," so you could imagine how silly it would sound to say "*Me gusta los coches*" or "*Nos gustan bailar.*"

¡Ojo! If the subject of the verb *gustar* or *encantar* is an infinitive (verb – *bailar, leer,* etc.), even if there are multiple verbs as the subject, the convention is to use the singular form of *gustar* (*gusta*) or *encantar* (*encanta*).

Ej. Me encanta~~n~~ correr y nadar.
Nos gusta~~n~~ bailar y cantar.

Las preguntas – Questions

In English, there are several cues that tell us a sentence is a question: it starts with an interrogative word (who, what, why, etc.) and/or the subject/verb order is flipped, or the word "do" is added.

Ej. *How* <u>are you</u>? (<u>You are</u> …) – subject/verb order was flipped, with question word
<u>Are you</u> impatient? (<u>You are</u> impatient.) – subject/verb order was flipped
<u>Do</u> you have a minute? (You have a minute.) – "do" was added to the beginning

In Spanish, there are also several cues that tell us it's a question, but they aren't all the same as the ones in English. Starting with an interrogative word (*quién, qué, por qué,* etc.) and/or flipping the subject/verb order is the same, but there isn't a word like "do" that we can add to the beginning. Instead, an upside-down question mark is placed at the beginning of the question (not necessarily the beginning of the sentence). This is done for all questions, regardless of the other cues.

Ej. ¿*Cómo* <u>estás tú</u>? (<u>Tú estás</u> …) – subject/verb order was switched, with question word
¿<u>Eres tú</u> impaciente? (<u>Tú eres</u> impaciente.) – subject/verb order was switched
¿<u>Trabajas</u>? (Trabajas.) – The upside-down question mark is like "do."

Unidad 3

Los verbos regulares (el presente) – Regular Verbs (present tense)

You have already been introduced to many common verbs, within the context of what you like to do, by using the verbs *gustar* and *encantar*. All of the verbs were presented to you in their infinitive form. Remember: according to Webster, an infinitive is a verb form having the characteristics of both verb and noun. In English, it is usually used with the word *to*: *to walk*, *to swim*, etc. According to yours truly, it is the most basic and root form of a verb. To conjugate a verb is to change it so that the resulting form agrees with the subject.

> *Ej.* I walk. You walk. She walks. I swim. You swim. She swims.

In Spanish, unlike in the above examples, each subject (1st person, singular; 1st person, plural; 2nd person, singular; 2nd person, plural; 3rd person, singular; and 3rd person, plural), in most tenses, has a unique verb conjugation.

All verbs in Spanish fall into one of three categories, which is determined by their endings in the infinitive form: *-ar, -er, -ir*. Within each category, verbs are classified, within the given tense, as either regular or irregular. All regular verbs follow the same rules of conjugation for their respective category (regular *-ar*, regular *-er*, and regular *-ir*). Irregular verbs do not follow the same rules and their conjugations must be learned individually. Fortunately for learners of Spanish as a foreign language, most verbs are regular in their conjugations. Take a look at the following example of a regular present-tense *-ar* verb.

	singular		plural			singular		plural	
	hablar					**to speak**			
1st person	yo	**habl**o	nosotros	**habl**amos		I	speak	we	speak
2nd person	tú	**habl**as	vosotros	**habl**áis		you	speak	you	speak
3rd person	él / ella / usted (Ud.)	**habl**a	ellos / ellas / ustedes (Uds.)	**habl**an		he / she	speaks	they	speak

Notice that the stem of the verb (everything but the ending) does not change, only the ending. To conjugate regular verbs, you simply drop the infinitive ending: *-ar, -er, -ir*; and then add the corresponding conjugated ending.

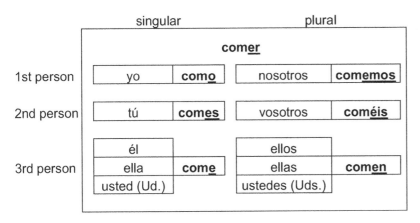

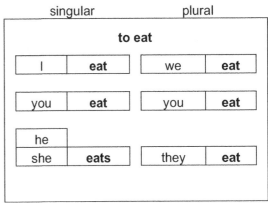

¡Ojo! *Usted* and *ustedes* are 2nd person, formal, but they are conjugated as 3rd person.

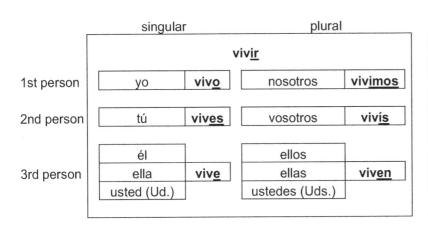

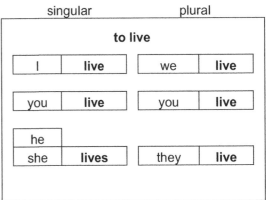

¡Ojo! The *vosotros* form is used primarily in Spain. In Latin America, *ustedes* serves as both the familiar and formal forms of *you, plural*.

La posesión y los adjetivos posesivos – Possession and Possessive Adjectives

mi(s) – my	**nuestro(s)** / **nuestra(s)** – our
tu(s) – your	**vuestro(s)** / **vuestra(s)** – your (Spain plural)
su(s) – his / her / your (formal)	**su(s)** – their / your (Latin America plural, formal)
de – of (used to clarify 3rd person)	

Ej. mi amigo – my friend
   mi<u>s</u> amigo<u>s</u> – my friends
   nuestr<u>o</u> maestr<u>o</u> – our (male) teacher
   nuestr<u>a</u> maestr<u>a</u> – our (female) teacher
   nuestr<u>os</u> maestr<u>os</u> – our (male, or male and female) teachers
   la calculadora <u>de mi jefe</u> – <u>my boss's</u> calculator (literally – the calculator <u>of my boss</u>)
   La maestra <u>de mi amiga</u> es amable. – <u>My friend's</u> teacher is kind.

Unidad 4

Los verbos irregulares (el presente) – Irregular Verbs (present tense)

You have already been introduced to regular present-tense verbs. There are two parts to every verb in Spanish: the stem and the ending. By definition, all regular verbs retain the stem of their infinitives and only their endings change.

habl<u>ar</u>	com<u>er</u>	viv<u>ir</u>
habl<u>o</u>	com<u>o</u>	viv<u>o</u>
habl<u>as</u>	com<u>es</u>	viv<u>es</u>
habl<u>a</u>	com<u>e</u>	viv<u>e</u>
habl<u>amos</u>	com<u>emos</u>	viv<u>imos</u>
habl<u>áis</u>	com<u>éis</u>	viv<u>ís</u>
habl<u>an</u>	com<u>en</u>	viv<u>en</u>

Irregular verbs do not follow these rules and their conjugations must be learned individually. There are several different types of irregular verbs; some are stem-changing verbs (which can be categorized by the type of change required); some change, remove, or add letters to retain their pronunciation; and some don't seem to follow any pattern at all. Take a look at the following examples of some irregular present-tense verbs. Notice the types of stem changes in parentheses.

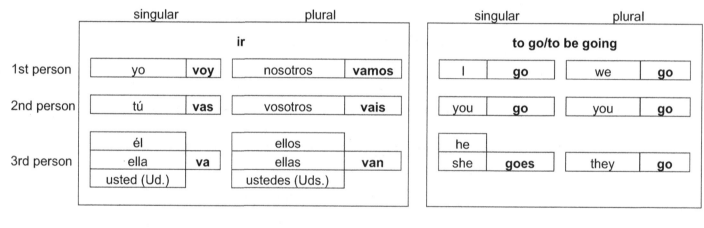

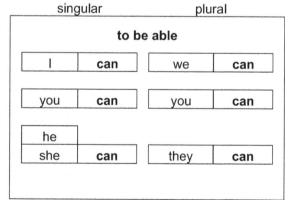

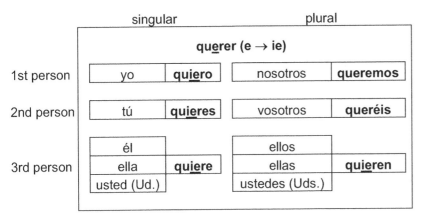
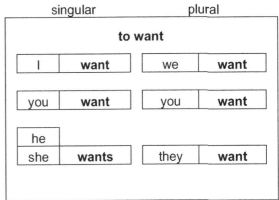

¡Ojo! Usted and *ustedes* are 2nd person, formal, but they are conjugated as 3rd person.

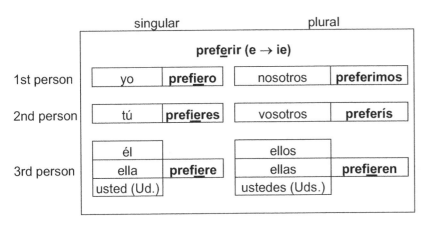
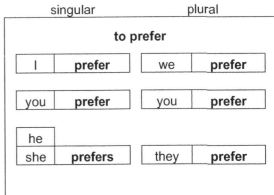

¡Ojo! The *vosotros* form is used primarily in Spain. In Latin America, *ustedes* serves as both the familiar and formal forms of *you, plural*.

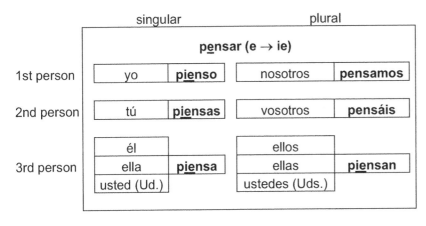
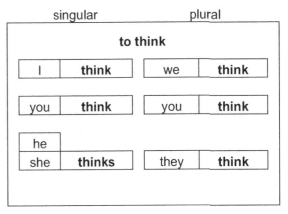

Sometimes the *yo* form has a unique change.

Ej. **ver** (to see / to watch) – yo ~~vo~~ **veo**   **dar** (to give) – yo ~~do~~ **doy**
    saber (to know) – yo ~~sabo~~ **sé**   **hacer** (to do / to make) – yo ~~haco~~ **hago**

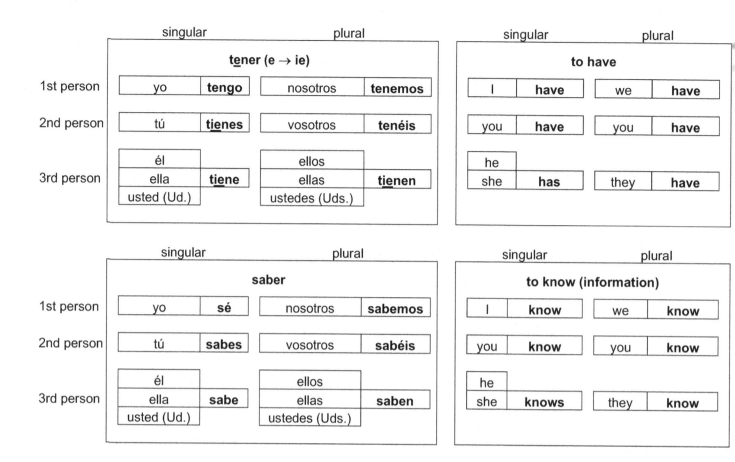

Los infinitivos y las estructuras compuestas – Infinitives and Compound Structures

Many verbs can be combined with infinitives to form compound structures. Take a look at the following examples below. Each conjugated verb can be conjugated according to any subject, but the second verb remains in the infinitive form no matter who the subject may be. I have included a few prepositions that signal the use of an infinitive as well.

Tengo que estudiar. – I have to study.

Quiero comer. – I want to eat.

¿Prefieres correr? – Do you prefer to run?

Necesitan intentar. – They need to try.

¿Puedo ir al baño? – Can I go to the bathroom?

Sabe manejar. – He knows how to drive.

Vamos a viajar. – We are going to travel.

Pienso viajar. – I plan to travel.

Intentan nadar. – They try to swim.

para estudiar – in order to study

después de leer – after reading

antes de nadar – before swimming

Notice that the verb structure *ir + a* + infinitive is one form of the future tense. Other verbs structures that can imply the future are *necesitar* + infinitive, *querer* + infinitive, and *pensar* + infinitive.

Unidad 5

Los verbos (el presente) – Verbs (present tense)

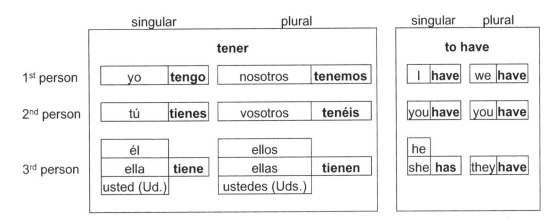

¡Ojo! *Usted* and *ustedes* are 2nd person, formal, but they are conjugated as 3rd person.

	singular		plural	
	tener			
1st person	yo	**tengo**	nosotros	**tenemos**
2nd person	tú	**tienes**	vosotros	**tenéis**
3rd person	él / ella / usted (Ud.)	**tiene**	ellos / ellas / ustedes (Uds.)	**tienen**

	singular	plural
	to have	
1st person	I **have**	we **have**
2nd person	you **have**	you **have**
3rd person	he / she **has**	they **have**

¡Ojo! The *vosotros* form is used primarily in Spain. In Latin America, *ustedes* serves as both the familiar and formal forms of *you, plural.*

You have already seen the verb *tener* in context.
   Ej. ¿Cuántos años tienes? Tengo 34 años.

The idiomatic expression *tener años* means *to be years old* and it cannot be translated literally without losing meaning, which is the nature of idiomatic expressions. Some examples of other idiomatic expressions using the verb *tener* are:

tener frío – to be cold	Tengo frío. – I am cold.
tener calor – to be hot	¿Tienes calor? – Are you hot?
tener sueño – to be sleepy	Mi hija tiene sueño. – My daughter is sleepy.
tener sed – to be thirsty	Tenemos sed. – We are thirsty.
tener hambre – to be hungry	¿Tienen hambre? – Are you (all) hungry?
tener miedo – to be afraid	Tengo miedo. – I am afraid.
tener prisa – to be in a hurry	Tenemos prisa. – We are in a hurry.

Unidad 6

Los adjetivos – Adjectives

You've been introduced to the concept of adjectives having gender and number as well as agreeing with the nouns they modify (p.7). They can be used with the verbs *ser* and *estar*.

> *Ej.* El carro es <u>negro</u>.　　　　　Las casas son <u>pequeñas</u>.
> La comida está <u>fría</u>.　　　　　Mis amigos están <u>enfermos</u>.

They can also be used without *ser* or *estar*. Remember that adjectives almost always follow the nouns they modify. You can also use more than one adjective to describe the same noun.

> *Ej.* Yo prefiero el carro <u>negro</u> y <u>amarillo</u>.　　No me gustan las casas <u>pequeñas</u>.

Don't be thrown off by words like *persona* or *masculino/a* and *femenino/a*; just follow the rules.

> *Ej.* Juan es un<u>a</u> person<u>a</u> atractiv<u>a</u>.　　　"Problema" es un<u>a</u> palab<u>ra</u> masculina.

Los adverbios – Adverbs

Adjectives modify nouns, whereas adverbs modify verbs (and adjectives). Nouns have gender and number, therefore adjectives have corresponding gender and number. Verbs, on the other hand, do not have gender or number, therefore adverbs, likewise, do not have gender or number.

> *Ej.* Mi hermana juega <u>bien.</u>　　　Nuestros tíos cantan <u>mal</u>.
> Mi hermano juega <u>bien.</u>　　　Nuestra tía canta <u>mal</u>.

In English, we can add "ly" to many adjectives to turn them into adverbs. Likewise, in Spanish, we can add *-mente* to the **feminine** form of many adjectives to make adverbs.

> *Ej.* quick　→　quick<u>ly</u>　　　　　rápid**a** → rápida<u>mente</u>
> sincere → sincere<u>ly</u>　　　　sincero/**a** → sincera<u>mente</u>
> simple → simp<u>ly</u>　　　　　simple　→　simple<u>mente</u>
> formal → formal<u>ly</u>　　　　formal　→　formal<u>mente</u>

Los comparativos – Comparatives

Comparatives, as the name implies, make comparisons between two things either with adjectives or adverbs. In the case of adjectives, the adjectives in question do not modify both nouns; they only modify the first one. In the case of adverbs, there is no issue.

> *Ej.* Mi tí<u>o</u> es *más* alt<u>o</u> *que* mi papá.　　Tu herman<u>a</u> es *más* cariños<u>a</u> *que* tu prima.
> Mi tí<u>o</u> es *más* alt<u>o</u> *que* mi mamá.　　Tu herman<u>a</u> es *más* cariños<u>a</u> *que* tus primos.
>
> Mi hermano corre *más* rápidamente *que* <u>yo</u>. (more quickly than <u>I do/me</u>)
> Nuestros primos corren *más* rápidamente *que* <u>nosotros</u>. (more quickly than <u>we do/us</u>)

¡Ojo! In English, we often use "me/I," "us/we," and "them/they" interchangeably. This is not the case in Spanish. For these comparatives, always use subject pronouns (*yo, tú, él/ella*, etc.).

Unidad 7

Los pronombres de complemento directo – Direct-Object Pronouns

lo – it (masculine)	**la** – it (feminine)
los – them (masculine / masculine and feminine)	**las** – them (feminine)

As in English, pronouns (*pronombres*) in Spanish are used to replace nouns (*sustantivos*). What is different from English is their placement with respect to the verb: before a conjugated verb or attached to an infinitive.

Ej. ¿Quieres <u>la blusa</u>?   ¿Tienes <u>los pantalones</u>?
  No, no <u>la</u> quiero. – No, I don't want <u>it</u>. Sí, <u>los</u> tengo. – Yes, I have <u>them</u>.

  ¿Quieres llevar <u>esta corbata</u>?
  No, no <u>la</u> quiero llevar.   or   No, no quiero llevar<u>la</u>.

Las preguntas – Questions

There are several phrases you can use to ask people how they like something (food, clothing, etc.). Your inclination is probably to translate the word "how" as *cómo* and finish it off with the verb *gustar*. This would make sense in Spanish, but it probably would not mean what you think.

  Ej. ¿Cómo te gusta tu café? – How do you like (prefer) your coffee?
  Me gusta mi café con leche. – I like (prefer) my coffee with milk.

To inquire about someone's experience with a specific thing, use the verb *estar* with *cómo*.

  Ej. ¿Cómo está tu café? – How is your coffee?
  Mi café está caliente pero muy bueno. – My coffee is hot, but very good (tasty).

To ask someone's opinion of a specific thing, use the verb *parecer* with *qué*.

  Ej. ¿Qué te parece esta camisa? – How does this shirt seem (look) to you?
  Esa camisa me parece muy bonita. – That shirt seems (looks) very pretty to me.

The phrase *¿qué tal?* is quite versatile. By itself it translates best as "How are things?" Even though it's not a verb, you can use it with an object to ask how it is.

  Ej. ¿Qué tal la sopa? – How's the soup? / How about the soup?
  La sopa está deliciosa. – The soup is delicious.

You can also use it in conjunction with verbs like *gustar*, *estar*, *parecer*, etc., which then translates to "how" in the way that *cómo* couldn't in the first example of this section.

  Ej. ¿Qué tal te gusta tu café?
  ¿Qué tal te parecen estos pantalones?
  ¿Qué tal está tu burrito?

Unidad 8

El presente progresivo – Progressive Present

The present tense is most often used to describe habitual action, and words like *siempre, nunca, todos los días, de vez en cuando*, etc. describe the frequency of that action. The present tense can also be used to describe ongoing action that is taking place in the moment (right now).

This construction has two components: the verb *estar*, conjugated in the present tense, and the gerund form (-ing) of the action verb. This is called the progressive present.

> *Ej.* ¿Qué **estás** hac*iendo*? – What **are you** do*ing*?
> **Estoy** desayun*ando*. – **I am** eat*ing* breakfast.

Review the verb *estar* in the present tense and notice the construction of the gerund (-ing).

estar – to be		-ing
estoy	estamos	-ar → -ando
estás	estáis	-er → -iendo
está	están	-ir → -iendo

¡Ojo! The verb *estar* is conjugated in the present tense according to the subject of the action. The action verb in the gerund (-ing) is not conjugated; it is an adverb, which has no subject or gender.

> *Ej.* **Estoy** jug*ando*. – **I am** play*ing*.   **Estamos** jug*ando*. – **We are** play*ing*.
> **Estás** jug*ando*. – **You are** play*ing*.   **Estáis** jug*ando*. – **You (all) are** play*ing*.
> **Está** jug*ando*. – **S/he is** play*ing*.   **Están** jug*ando*. – **They are** play*ing*.
>
> **Estoy** com*iendo*. – **I am** eat*ing*.   **Estamos** com*iendo*. – **We are** eat*ing*.
> **Estás** com*iendo*. – **You are** eat*ing*.   **Estáis** com*iendo*. – **You (all) are** eat*ing*.
> **Está** com*iendo*. – **S/he is** eat*ing*.   **Están** com*iendo*. – **They are** eat*ing*.
>
> **Estoy** escrib*iendo*. – **I am** writ*ing*.   **Estamos** escrib*iendo*. – **We are** writ*ing*.
> **Estás** escrib*iendo*. – **You are** writ*ing*.   **Estáis** escrib*iendo*. – **You (all) are** writ*ing*.
> **Está** escrib*iendo*. – **S/he is** writ*ing*.   **Están** escrib*iendo*. – **They are** writ*ing*.

- **The gerund: noun or adverb?**

In English, the gerund (-ing) form can be either a noun or an adverb.
> *Ej.* Running (noun) is good for you.   She spends her days dreaming (adverb).

In Spanish, the gerund form can only be used as an adverb. If you want the noun form for -ing, use the infinitive. This means the infinitive is used as the subject of another verb as well as after a preposition (*por, para, sin, con, de*, etc.) whether the translation to English is "to __" or "__ing."

> *Ej.* ~~Corriendo~~ Corr*er* es bueno para ti.   Ella pasa sus días soñ*ando* (adverbio).
> Me gusta ~~corriendo~~ correr. – I like <u>to run</u>. / I like <u>running</u>.
> sin correr – without running, después de comer – after eating

Unidad 9

Los verbos irregulares (el presente) – Irregular Verbs (present tense)

You should already be familiar with the concept of stem-changing verbs. Here is a review of two irregular verbs that we have already studied.

tener (e → ie) – to have			
yo	tengo	nosotros	tenemos
tú	tienes	vosotros	tenéis
él / ella / usted (Ud.)	tiene	ellos / ellas / ustedes (Uds.)	tienen

preferir (e → ie) – to prefer			
yo	prefiero	nosotros	preferimos
tú	prefieres	vosotros	preferís
él / ella / usted (Ud.)	prefiere	ellos / ellas / ustedes (Uds.)	prefieren

Notice that *tener* has a unique change in the 1st person, singular form (*yo*). Here are two more verbs that have a similar change in the 1st person, singular form in the present, but the rest of the conjugations are regular.

hacer – to do / to make			
yo	hago	nosotros	hacemos
tú	haces	vosotros	hacéis
él / ella / usted (Ud.)	hace	ellos / ellas / ustedes (Uds.)	hacen

poner – to put / to place / to set			
yo	pongo	nosotros	ponemos
tú	pones	vosotros	ponéis
él / ella / usted (Ud.)	pone	ellos / ellas / ustedes (Uds.)	ponen

The verb *hay* is a very useful word. It means *there is* or *there are* and can be used in similar situations as the verb *tener*. Whereas *tener,* when conjugated, has a subject, and therefore tells us who possesses a certain item, *hay* is generic and is used when it is not necessary to express who an item or items belong to.

> *Ej.* **Yo tengo** una cama en mi habitación.
> **I have** a bed in my bedroom.
>
> **Hay** una cama en mi habitación.
> **There is** a bed in my bedroom.

Los pronombres de complemento directo – Direct-Object Pronouns

lo – it (masculine)	**la** – it (feminine)
los – them (masculine / masculine and feminine)	**las** – them (feminine)

As in English, pronouns (*pronombres*) in Spanish are used to replace nouns (*sustantivos*). What is different from English is their placement with respect to the verb.

> *Ej.* How often do you <u>clean</u> **the bathroom**?
> I <u>clean</u> **it** every Saturday.
>
> ¿Con qué frecuencia <u>limpias</u> **el baño**?
> Yo **lo** <u>limpio</u> todos los sábados.

Notice that *el baño* is a masculine noun and therefore it is replaced with the appropriate masculine, singular pronoun: *lo*.

Also notice that in Spanish, the pronoun comes immediately before the conjugated verb whereas in English, the pronoun comes after the verb. When you have two verbs in Spanish, one conjugated (*prefiero*) and one in its infinitive form (*limpiar*), the pronoun has two correct placements.

> *Ej.* Do you <u>prefer</u> <u>to clean</u> **the kitchen** tonight or tomorrow night?
> I <u>prefer</u> <u>to clean</u> **it** tonight.
>
> ¿<u>Prefieres</u> <u>limpiar</u> **la cocina** esta noche o mañana por la noche?
> Yo **la** <u>prefiero</u> <u>limpiar</u> esta noche.

Notice that in the above example, the feminine pronoun (*la*) replaces the feminine noun (*la cocina*) and is correctly placed directly before the conjugated verb *prefiero*. Below, we will see its alternate placement: attached to the end of the infinitive.

> *Ej.* ¿<u>Prefieres</u> <u>limpiar</u> **la cocina** esta noche o mañana por la noche?
> Yo <u>prefiero</u> <u>limpiar</u>**la** esta noche.

Both of these placements are equally correct and there is no specific preference in either case; usually the placement will be determined by the speaker/writer based on whichever one rolls off the tongue most easily. Again, we only have this option when we have both a conjugated verb and an infinitive together. If we *only* have a conjugated verb (*limpio*), the pronoun *must* be placed directly before the verb. If we *only* have an infinitive (*limpiar*), the pronoun *must* be attached to the end of the verb.

> *Ej.* Voy a la cocina para <u>limpiar</u>**la**.
> **La** <u>limpio</u> después de <u>usar</u>**la**.

Unidad 10

Los verbos irregulares (el presente) – Irregular Verbs (present tense)

Here is a review of some irregular verbs.

tener (e → ie) – to have			
yo	**tengo**	nosotros	**tenemos**
tú	**tienes**	vosotros	**tenéis**
él / ella / usted (Ud.)	**tiene**	ellos / ellas / ustedes (Uds.)	**tienen**

pensar (e → ie) – to think			
yo	**pienso**	nosotros	**pensamos**
tú	**piensas**	vosotros	**pensáis**
él / ella / usted (Ud.)	**piensa**	ellos / ellas / ustedes (Uds.)	**piensan**

The following two verbs both mean *to be* in English but they have separate uses in Spanish.

- **Estar**: emotions, physical or mental states of being, and location
  (These circumstances can change frequently, from day to day or moment to moment.)

  Ej. Yo <u>estoy</u> contento. – I am happy. (emotion)
  Tú <u>estás</u> enfermo. – You are sick. (physical state of being)
  Ella <u>está</u> loca. – She is crazy. (mental state of being)
  Nosotros <u>estamos</u> en clase. – We are in class. (location)

- **Ser**: origins, time, days, dates, professions, physical characteristics, and personality traits
  (These characteristics are usually permanent, but may change over long periods of time.)

  Ej. Yo <u>soy</u> de Colorado. – I am from Colorado. (origin)
  Hoy <u>es</u> sábado. – Today is Saturday. (days)
  Ella <u>es</u> médica. – She is a doctor. (profession)
  Nosotros <u>somos</u> altos. – We are tall. (physical characteristic)
  Ellos <u>son</u> simpáticos. – They are nice. (personality trait)

estar – to be			
yo	**estoy**	nosotros	**estamos**
tú	**estás**	vosotros	**estáis**
él / ella / usted (Ud.)	**está**	ellos / ellas / ustedes (Uds.)	**están**

ser – to be			
yo	**soy**	nosotros	**somos**
tú	**eres**	vosotros	**sois**
él / ella / usted (Ud.)	**es**	ellos / ellas / ustedes (Uds.)	**son**

Los pronombres de complemento indirecto – Indirect-Object Pronouns

me – me	**nos** – us
te – you	**os** – you (Spain plural)
le – him / her / you (formal)	**les** – them / you (Latin America plural, formal)

You have studied the verbs *gustar* and *encantar*, which, when translated into English, cause problems between subject and object.

English: "I like the class." – "I" is the subject and "the class" is the object.
Spanish: "The class pleases me." – "The class" is the subject and "me" is the object.

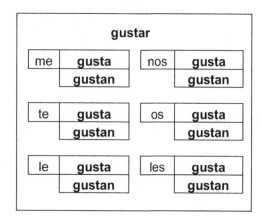 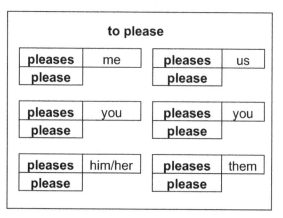

Another verb that follows a similar pattern is the verb *doler* (to ache/to hurt). It is used with body parts and is almost always conjugated in the 3rd person: singular (one body <u>part</u> that <u>hurts</u>) or plural (multiple body <u>parts</u> that <u>hurt</u>). **The indirect object (pronoun) indicates the person whose body part(s) hurt(s) and is completely independent of the conjugation of the verb _doler_.**

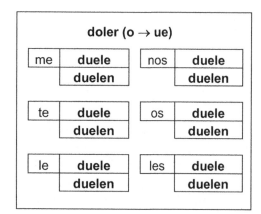 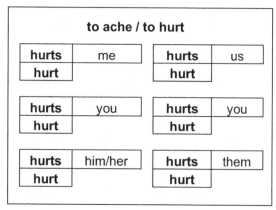

Ej. Me duele la rodilla. – My knee hurts.   ¿Te duele la rodilla? – Does your knee hurt?
     Me duelen las rodillas. – My knees hurt. ¿Te duelen las rodillas? Do your knees hurt?

¡Ojo! When separate singular nouns come after the verb, the verb can be either singular or plural.

Ej. Me duel<u>e</u> el estómago y la cabeza.   or   Me duel<u>en</u> el estómago y la cabeza.

Double Negatives

Negative words like *nunca, nada, nadie,* and *ninguno* have affirmative meanings, as well, so what looks like a double negative is really an affirmation of the negative.

> *Ej.* No lo hago *nunca.* – I don't *ever* do it.
> No nos gusta *ninguno.* – We don't like *any* (of them).
> No hay *nadie* aquí. – There isn't *anyone* here.
> No tiene *nada.* – She doesn't have *anything.*

Los verbos reflexivos – Reflexive Verbs

The subject of a sentence/phrase is the person or thing that does the action of the verb or is otherwise described by that verb if it is not an action.

> *Ej.* Yo llamo al médico cuando estoy enfermo. – I call the doctor when I am sick.

The object of a sentence/phrase is the person or thing that receives the benefit, consequence, effect, etc. of the verb either directly or indirectly.

> *Ej.* Yo llamo al médico cuando estoy enfermo. – I call the doctor when I am sick.
> Yo lo llamo cuando estoy enfermo. – I call him when I am sick.

When the subject and object of a sentence/phrase are the same person, the verb is considered reflexive. This means that the subject does an action to itself, for itself, etc. The most common use of reflexive verbs is for those describing one's daily routine (Unit 13). There are many other uses of reflexive verbs in Spanish and many do not translate well into English, so until you understand all of the subtle uses and meanings of reflexive verbs, you may just have to accept their conjugation rules as they are.

> *Ej.* Yo me llamo David. – I call myself David (my name is David).

Los pronombres reflexivos – Reflexive Pronouns

me – myself	**nos** – ourselves
te – yourself	**os** – yourselves (Spain plural)
se – himself / herself / yourself (formal)	**se** – themselves / yourselves (Latin America plural, formal)

A reflexive verb looks like any other verb, whether regular or irregular in any given verb tense, with the exception of the reflexive pronoun that accompanies it. It is this pronoun that makes the verb reflexive.

¡Ojo! The reflexive pronoun must match the subject in person (1st, 2nd, 3rd) and number (s., pl.).

Take a look at the following reflexive verbs in the **present tense** and notice that the reflexive pronouns match each subject and also notice their placement.

	singular		plural	
	llamarse – to call oneself			
1st person	yo	**me llamo**	nosotros	**nos llamamos**
2nd person	tú	**te llamas**	vosotros	**os llamáis**
3rd person	él / ella / usted (Ud.)	**se llama**	ellos / ellas / ustedes (Uds.)	**se llaman**

	singular		plural	
	sentirse (e → ie) – to feel			
1st person	yo	**me siento**	nosotros	**nos sentimos**
2nd person	tú	**te sientes**	vosotros	**os sentís**
3rd person	él / ella / usted (Ud.)	**se siente**	ellos / ellas / ustedes (Uds.)	**se sienten**

	singular		plural	
	quedarse – to stay / to remain			
1st person	yo	**me quedo**	nosotros	**nos quedamos**
2nd person	tú	**te quedas**	vosotros	**os quedáis**
3rd person	él / ella / usted (Ud.)	**se queda**	ellos / ellas / ustedes (Uds.)	**se quedan**

	singular		plural	
	mejorarse – to get better			
1st person	yo	me mejoro	nosotros	nos mejoramos
2nd person	tú	te mejoras	vosotros	os mejoráis
3rd person	él / ella / usted (Ud.)	se mejora	ellos / ellas / ustedes (Uds.)	se mejoran

	singular		plural	
	soplarse (la nariz) – to blow one's (nose)			
1st person	yo	me soplo	nosotros	nos soplamos
2nd person	tú	te soplas	vosotros	os sopláis
3rd person	él / ella / usted (Ud.)	se sopla	ellos / ellas / ustedes (Uds.)	se soplan

Reflexive pronouns follow the same placement rules as indirect-object pronouns (pp.11, 24) and direct-object pronouns (pp.19, 22) – immediately before a conjugated verb or attached to the end of an infinitive.

> *Ej.* Yo **me** siento fatal.
> Ella y yo **nos** sentimos fatal.
>
> Yo debo tomar mucha agua y descansar mucho para mejorar**me**.
> Ella y yo debemos tomar mucha agua y descansar mucho para mejorar**nos**.

When there are two verbs together, one conjugated (*debo*) and one in its infinitive form (*quedarse*), the speaker/writer has an option with respect to the placement of the pronoun.

> *Ej.* Me debo quedar en la cama. (immediately before the conjugated verb)
> Debo quedarme en la cama. (attached to the end of the infinitive)

Unidad 11

Los verbos (el pretérito) – Verbs (preterite/past tense)

In Spanish, as in most languages, there are many different verb tenses. So far, we have only studied the present tense although you may have seen or heard other tenses before. It is time to expand on your understanding of verb tenses by introducing one of the past tenses: the preterite. This tense is used to talk about events that happened at a specific time or a specific number of times in the past. Some words that would signal the preterite are the following:

ayer – yesterday
anteayer – the day before yesterday
anoche – last night
el sábado pasado – last Saturday

la semana pasada – last week
el año pasado – last year
hace dos días – two days ago
hace tres semanas – three weeks ago

As you already know, all verbs in Spanish fall into one of three categories, which is determined by their endings in the infinitive form: -ar, -er, -ir. Within each category, verbs are classified, within the given tense, as either regular or irregular. All regular verbs follow the same rules of conjugation for their respective category (regular -ar, regular -er, and regular -ir). Irregular verbs do not follow the same rules and their conjugations must be learned individually. It is important to understand that each tense has unique endings. Take a look at the following example of a regular preterite-tense -ar verb. Notice the differences from the present, especially accent marks.

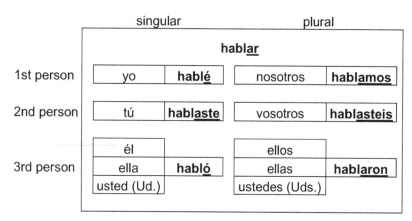
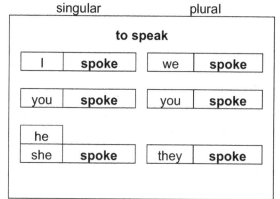

Notice that the stem of the verb (everything but the ending) does not change, only the ending. To conjugate regular verbs, you simply drop the infinitive ending: -ar, -er, -ir; and add the corresponding conjugated ending.

¡Ojo! The *nosotros* forms for -ar and -ir verbs are the same in the present and the preterite tenses. The only way to determine whether the conjugation is present or preterite is by understanding the context of the sentence; key words/phrases such as *todos los días* and *ayer* are the biggest indicators.

singular		plural		singular		plural	
comer				**to eat**			
yo	**comí**	nosotros	**comimos**	I	ate	we	ate
tú	**comiste**	vosotros	**comisteis**	you	ate	you	ate
él		ellos		he			
ella	**comió**	ellas	**comieron**	she	ate	they	ate
usted (Ud.)		ustedes (Uds.)					

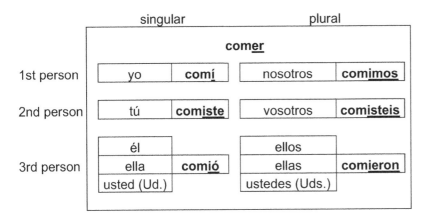
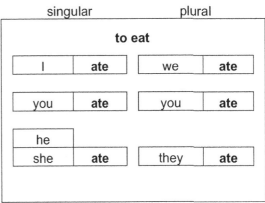

¡Ojo! Usted and *ustedes* are 2nd person, formal, but they are conjugated as 3rd person.

singular		plural		singular		plural	
vivir				**to live**			
yo	**viví**	nosotros	**vivimos**	I	lived	we	lived
tú	**viviste**	vosotros	**vivisteis**	you	lived	you	lived
él		ellos		he			
ella	**vivió**	ellas	**vivieron**	she	lived	they	lived
usted (Ud.)		ustedes (Uds.)					

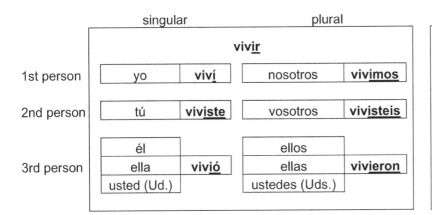
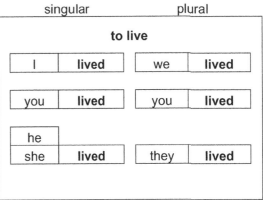

¡Ojo! The *vosotros* form is used primarily in Spain. In Latin America, *ustedes* serves as both the familiar and formal forms of *you, plural.*

Take a look at the following sentences that contrast the present tense with the preterite tense. Notice the key words/phrases that signal frequency.

> *Ej.* Mónica **generalmente** come en casa, pero **ayer**, comió en un restaurante.
>
> Les <u>gusta</u> jugar al béisbol durante el verano, pero **el verano pasado**, no <u>jugaron</u>.
>
> **Normalmente**, <u>estudiamos</u> en la biblioteca, pero **ayer**, <u>estudiamos</u> en la cafetería.

Los verbos irregulares (el pretérito) – Irregular Verbs (preterite/past tense)

Just like the present tense, the preterite tense has irregular verbs. Some irregular verbs in the present are also irregular in the preterite, but not always. No verb is inherently irregular; their irregularities are tense specific. We will study a few different types of preterite irregulars in the next unit, but for now, here are a few common ones to get you started.

¡Ojo! These irregular verbs in the preterite tense do not have accent marks.

Notice that *ir* and *ser* have the same conjugations in the preterite but their meanings remain different. The way to determine whether a conjugation is from the verb *ir* or *ser*, you must understand the context of the sentence.

Ej. Fue al cine el sábado pasado.
He went to the movies last Saturday. vs. He ~~was~~ to the movies last Saturday.

Ej. Mi abuelo fue ingeniero.
My grandpa was an engineer. vs. My grandpa ~~went~~ an engineer.

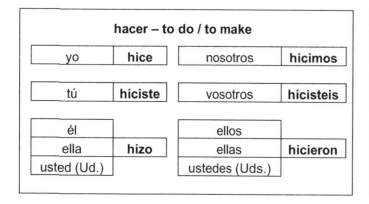

Notice the spelling change from *c* to *z* in the 3rd person, singular category (*él, ella, Ud.*).

Unidad 12

Los verbos irregulares (el presente) – Irregular Verbs (present tense)

You should now be aware that there are different types of irregular verbs. Some require a stem change (*poder*, *querer*), while others require a complete change (*ser*, *ir*). There are also some that have a unique change in the 1st person, singular form *yo* (*hacer*, *tener*). Take a look at some other irregular verbs that follow this pattern and notice the unique changes with *yo*.

poner – to put / to place / to set			
yo	pongo	nosotros	ponemos
tú	pones	vosotros	ponéis
él / ella / usted (Ud.)	pone	ellos / ellas / ustedes (Uds.)	ponen

hacer – to do / to make			
yo	hago	nosotros	hacemos
tú	haces	vosotros	hacéis
él / ella / usted (Ud.)	hace	ellos / ellas / ustedes (Uds.)	hacen

tener (e → ie) – to have			
yo	tengo	nosotros	tenemos
tú	tienes	vosotros	tenéis
él / ella / usted (Ud.)	tiene	ellos / ellas / ustedes (Uds.)	tienen

salir – to go out / to leave			
yo	salgo	nosotros	salimos
tú	sales	vosotros	salís
él / ella / usted (Ud.)	sale	ellos / ellas / ustedes (Uds.)	salen

traer – to bring			
yo	traigo	nosotros	traemos
tú	traes	vosotros	traéis
él / ella / usted (Ud.)	trae	ellos / ellas / ustedes (Uds.)	traen

venir (e → ie) – to come			
yo	vengo	nosotros	venimos
tú	vienes	vosotros	venís
él / ella / usted (Ud.)	viene	ellos / ellas / ustedes (Uds.)	vienen

Conocer vs. saber

You may have studied the verb *saber* before, but you may not have realized that there is another verb with the same translation to English: *conocer*. Both mean "to know" in English, but each has a unique use in Spanish.

- **Conocer**

Conocer is used when talking about personal experiences that cannot be summarized by mere facts. To know someone personally is a much more abstract concept than to simply know details about that same person. *Conocer*, however, is not limited to people; it can also refer to anything you can be familiar with: a place, a song, a feeling, etc.

> *Ej. Mi mamá **conoce** a tu amiga.* (personally)

> *¿**Conoces** muy bien la ciudad de Denver?* (personally)

¡Ojo! – The *a* in the first example, right before *tu amiga*, is called the "personal *a*" and is used to distinguish the subject of the sentence from the direct object of the sentence when the direct object is a person.

- **Saber**

Saber, in contrast, is used when talking about details, facts or other information that can answer the questions *¿quién? ¿cuándo? ¿dónde? ¿por qué? ¿cómo? ¿cuánto? ¿qué?* and *¿cuál?*

> *Ej. Mi mamá **sabe** quién es tu amiga.* (information)

> *¿**Sabes** dónde está Alejandra?* (information)

As with the verbs on the previous page, *saber* and *conocer* in the present tense have unique changes in the 1st person, singular form *yo*.

conoc**er** – to know (personally)			
yo	**conozco**	nosotros	**conocemos**
tú	**conoces**	vosotros	**conocéis**
él / ella / usted (Ud.)	**conoce**	ellos / ellas / ustedes (Uds.)	**conocen**

saber – to know (information)			
yo	**sé**	nosotros	**sabemos**
tú	**sabes**	vosotros	**sabéis**
él / ella / usted (Ud.)	**sabe**	ellos / ellas / ustedes (Uds.)	**saben**

Los verbos irregulares (el pretérito) – Irregular Verbs (preterite/past tense)

You have already been introduced to regular preterite-tense verbs. There are two parts to every verb in Spanish: the stem and the ending. By definition, all regular verbs retain the stem of their infinitives and only their endings change.

habl**ar**	com**er**	viv**ir**
habl**é**	com**í**	viv**í**
habl**aste**	com**iste**	viv**iste**
habl**ó**	com**ió**	viv**ió**
habl**amos**	com**imos**	viv**imos**
habl**asteis**	com**isteis**	viv**isteis**
habl**aron**	com**ieron**	viv**ieron**

As you know, irregular verbs do not follow these rules and their conjugations must be learned individually. What you may not know yet is that *irregular* is verb-tense specific. That means that irregular verbs in the present are not necessarily irregular in the preterite or any other verb tense for that matter. As in the present tense, there are several different types of irregular verbs; some are stem-changing verbs (which can be categorized by the type of change required), some change, remove, or add letters to retain their pronunciation, and some don't seem to follow any pattern at all. Take a look at the following examples of some irregular present-tense verbs and compare them with their preterite-tense conjugations.

Notice that the preterite of *jugar* in the 1st person, singular form requires a *u* before the ending to maintain the proper pronunciation of the hard *g* sound. This change is coincidental and has nothing to do with the fact that *jugar* is irregular in the present tense. This change is required for all verbs ending in *gar*. Verbs ending in *car* and *zar* also require a spelling change in the 1st person, singular form in order to maintain correct pronunciation.

Ej. **sacar** – to take out
    yo **saqué**
    tú **sacaste**
    él **sacó**

comenzar – to start
    yo **comencé**
    tú **comenzaste**
    él **comenzó**

Verbs that end in *gar*, *car*, and *zar* have unique changes in the *yo* form in the preterite. This is due to the dual sounds of *g* and *c*. When followed by an *e* or *i*, *c* and *g* have a soft sound. When followed by an *a*, *o*, or *u*, they have a hard sound. In the case of the preterite, the *yo* form ending of *-ar* verbs is an *é*, which deviates from the other endings that start with either *a* or *o*. Take a look at the following pronunciation categories to better understand what's happening when we conjugate these *-gar*, *-car*, and *-zar* verbs in the preterite.

ga	gue		ja	ge / je		ca	que		za	ce
go	gui		jo	gi / ji		co	qui		zo	ci
gu			ju			cu			zu	

ju**g**o (Span.)   **j**u**g**o (Span.)   **c**olor (Span.)   **z**apato (Span.)
guess (Eng.)   **ha**ppy (Eng.)   **cu**t (Eng.)   **ce**lebrate (Eng.)

➤ The Spanish *g* can either sound similar to the English *g* (*golf*) or the English *h* depending on the letter that follows it.

➤ The Spanish *j* sounds similar to the English *h* regardless of the letter that follows it.

➤ The Spanish *c* sounds similar to the English *k* or the English *s* depending on the letter that follows it.

➤ The Spanish *z* sounds similar to the English *s* regardless of the letter that follows it. Note that the Spanish *z* is never pronounced like the English *z*; "zzzzzzz" no eggzzzzzziste.

The *yo* forms in the preterite are affected by these changes as are the preterite forms of *hacer*: hice (~~hize~~), hi**z**o (~~hico~~), but these pronunciation categories do not apply exclusively to verbs.

Ej. lápi**z** vs. lápi**c**es (*pencil*)   pe**z** vs. pe**c**es (*fish*)

Other pronunciation problems arise with *-eer* and *-aer* verbs in the preterite. In Spanish verbs, the vowel combinations *eio* and *aio* do not exist due to the weak pronunciation that would result, so *y* ("*i griega*" – "Greek i") substitutes for *i* ("*i*" or "*i latina*" – "i" or "Latin i") in the 3rd person conjugations to give them a stronger pronunciation. Notice the irregular accent marks.

leer – to read				
yo	leí		nosotros	leímos
tú	leíste		vosotros	leísteis
él			ellos	
ella	leyó		ellas	leyeron
usted (Ud.)			ustedes (Uds.)	

creer – to believe				
yo	creí		nosotros	creímos
tú	creíste		vosotros	creísteis
él			ellos	
ella	creyó		ellas	creyeron
usted (Ud.)			ustedes (Uds.)	

Los verbos irregulares (el pretérito) – Irregular Verbs (preterite/past tense)

As stated last unit (p.30), irregular verbs are tense specific. That said, there are some things we can observe that might help us identify irregulars from one tense to another. Take a look at some examples of stem-changing verbs in the present and what their preterite conjugations look like.

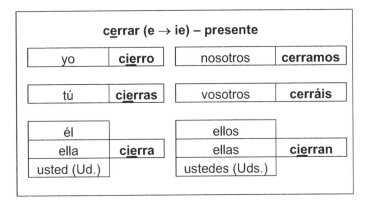

You can see that in the case of *cerrar* and *volver* above, the verbs are stem-changing in the present, but they are both regular in the preterite. This is typical both of *-ar* and *-er* verbs.

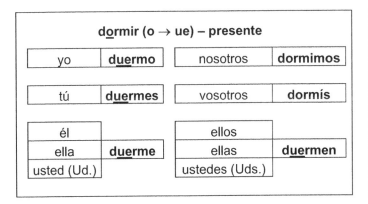

In the case of *-ir* verbs, stem-changing verbs in the present are irregular in the preterite and, in most cases, the preterite tense also requires a stem change in the 3rd person (*él / ellos*). Sometimes the stem changes are the same between tenses and sometimes they are different.

Unidad 13

Los verbos reflexivos – Reflexive Verbs

The <u>subject</u> of a sentence/phrase is the person or thing that does the action of the verb or is otherwise described by that verb if it is not an action.

> *Ej.* <u>Joaquín</u> lava el carro. – <u>Joaquin</u> washes the car.

The <u>object</u> of a sentence/phrase is the person or thing that receives the benefit, consequence, effect, etc. of the verb either directly or indirectly.

> *Ej.* Joaquín lava el <u>carro</u>. – Joaquin washes the <u>car</u>.

Of course, the <u>object</u> can be substituted with an <u>object pronoun</u> if the object in question has already been established (pp.19, 22).

> *Ej.* Joaquín <u>lo</u> lava. – Joaquin washes <u>it</u>.

When the <u>subject</u> and <u>object</u> of a sentence/phrase are the same person, the verb is considered reflexive. This means that the subject does an action to itself, for itself, etc. The most common use of reflexive verbs is for those describing one's daily routine. But there are many other uses of reflexive verbs in Spanish and many do not translate well into English. Until you understand all of the subtle uses and meanings of reflexive verbs, you may just have to accept their conjugation rules as they are.

> *Ej.* <u>Joaquín</u> <u>se</u> lava (el pelo). – <u>Joaquin</u> washes <u>himself</u> (his own hair).

Los pronombres reflexivos – Reflexive Pronouns

me – myself	**nos** – ourselves
te – yourself	**os** – yourselves (Spain plural)
se – himself / herself / yourself (formal)	**se** – themselves / yourselves (Latin America plural, formal)

A reflexive verb looks like any other verb, whether regular or irregular in any given verb tense, with the exception of the reflexive pronoun that accompanies it. It is this pronoun that makes the verb reflexive.

¡Ojo! The reflexive pronoun must match the subject in person (1st, 2nd, 3rd) and number (s., pl.).

Take a look at the following verbs in the **present tense** and notice the differences between the reflexive versions and the non-reflexive versions. Both are correct but have different meanings.

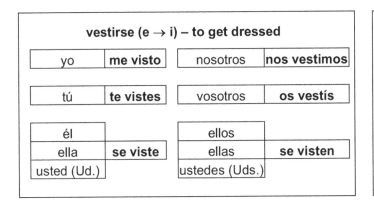

vestirse (e → i) – to get dressed			
yo	me visto	nosotros	nos vestimos
tú	te vistes	vosotros	os vestís
él / ella / usted (Ud.)	se viste	ellos / ellas / ustedes (Uds.)	se visten

vestir (e → i) – to dress (someone else)			
yo	visto	nosotros	vestimos
tú	vistes	vosotros	vestís
él / ella / usted (Ud.)	viste	ellos / ellas / ustedes (Uds.)	visten

Ej. <u>Yo</u> <u>me</u> visto. – I get dressed (I dress myself). – subject and object are the same

<u>Yo</u> visto <u>a mi hijo</u>. – I dress my son. – subject and object are different

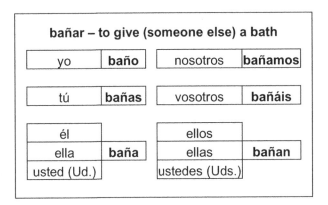

bañarse – to take a bath			
yo	me baño	nosotros	nos bañamos
tú	te bañas	vosotros	os bañáis
él / ella / usted (Ud.)	se baña	ellos / ellas / ustedes (Uds.)	se bañan

bañar – to give (someone else) a bath			
yo	baño	nosotros	bañamos
tú	bañas	vosotros	bañáis
él / ella / usted (Ud.)	baña	ellos / ellas / ustedes (Uds.)	bañan

Ej. <u>Yo</u> <u>me</u> baño. – I take a bath (I bathe myself). – subject and object are the same

<u>Yo</u> baño <u>a mi hijo</u>. – I give my son a bath. – subject and object are different

Reflexive pronouns follow the same placement rules as indirect-object pronouns (pp.11, 24) and direct-object pronouns (pp.19, 22) – immediately before a conjugated verb or attached to the end of an infinitive. When there are two verbs together, one conjugated (*voy*) and one in its infinitive form (*vestirse*), the speaker/writer has an option with respect to the placement of the pronoun.

Ej. <u>Me voy</u> a vestir en mi dormitorio. – I'm going to get dressed in my bedroom.

Voy a <u>vestirme</u> en mi dormitorio.

Todos los días, <u>me visto</u> en mi dormitorio después de <u>bañarme</u>.

Now take a look at the same verbs in the **preterite tense**. A verb can be reflexive regardless of its tense

vestirse (e → i) – to get dressed			
yo	**me vestí**	nosotros	**nos vestimos**
tú	**te vestiste**	vosotros	**os vestisteis**
él / ella / usted (Ud.)	**se vistió**	ellos / ellas / ustedes (Uds.)	**se vistieron**

vestir (e → i) – to dress (someone else)			
yo	**vestí**	nosotros	**vestimos**
tú	**vestiste**	vosotros	**vestisteis**
él / ella / usted (Ud.)	**vistió**	ellos / ellas / ustedes (Uds.)	**vistieron**

Ej. <u>Yo</u> <u>me</u> vestí. – I got dressed (I dressed myself). – subject and object are the same

<u>Yo</u> vestí <u>a mi hijo</u>. – I dressed my son. – subject and object are different

bañarse – to take a bath			
yo	**me bañé**	nosotros	**nos bañamos**
tú	**te bañaste**	vosotros	**os bañasteis**
él / ella / usted (Ud.)	**se bañó**	ellos / ellas / ustedes (Uds.)	**se bañaron**

bañar – to give (someone else) a bath			
yo	**bañé**	nosotros	**bañamos**
tú	**bañaste**	vosotros	**bañasteis**
él / ella / usted (Ud.)	**bañó**	ellos / ellas / ustedes (Uds.)	**bañaron**

Ej. <u>Yo</u> <u>me</u> bañé. – I took a bath (I bathed myself). – subject and object are the same

<u>Yo</u> bañé <u>a mi hijo</u>. – I gave my son a bath. – subject and object are different

Reflexive pronouns follow the same placement rules as indirect-object pronouns (pp.11, 24) and direct-object pronouns (pp.19, 22) – immediately before a conjugated verb or attached to the end of an infinitive. When there are two verbs together, one conjugated (*fui*) and one in its infinitive form (*vestirse*), the speaker/writer has an option with respect to the placement of the pronoun.

Ej. <u>Me fui</u> a vestir en mi dormitorio.

Fui a <u>vestirme</u> en mi dormitorio.

Ayer, <u>me vestí</u> en mi dormitorio después de <u>bañarme</u>.

Unidad 14

We have covered the concept of direct-object pronouns (pp.19, 22) and we have also covered reflexive pronouns (pp.25-27, 36-38), so let's review.

Los pronombres de complemento directo – Direct-Object Pronouns

lo – it (masculine)	**la** – it (feminine)
los – them (masculine / masculine and feminine)	**las** – them (feminine)

The best way to understand the use of direct objects is to think of them as answering the question *"what?"*

> *Ej.* Did you buy **the shirt**?
> Yes, I bought **it** last weekend.
>
> ¿Compraste la camisa?
> Sí, **la** compré el fin de semana pasado.

Notice that *la camisa* is a feminine noun and therefore it is replaced with the appropriate feminine, singular pronoun: *la*.

Also notice that in Spanish, the pronoun comes immediately before the conjugated verb whereas in English, the pronoun comes after the verb. When you have two verbs in Spanish, one conjugated (*voy*) and one in its infinitive form (*llevar*), the pronoun has two correct placements.

> *Ej.* Are you going to wear your new **suit** to the party?
> No, I'm going to wear **it** to church.
>
> ¿Vas a llevar tu **traje** nuevo a la fiesta?
> No, **lo** voy a llevar a la iglesia.

Notice that in the above example, the masculine pronoun (*lo*) replaced the masculine noun (*el traje*) and is correctly placed directly before the conjugated verb *voy*. Below, we will see its alternate placement: attached to the end of the infinitive.

> *Ej.* ¿Vas a llevar tu **traje** nuevo a la fiesta?
> No, voy a llevar**lo** a la iglesia.

Both of these placements are equally correct and there is no specific preference in either case; usually the placement will be determined by the speaker/writer based on whichever one rolls off the tongue the easiest. Again, we only have this option when we have both a conjugated verb and an infinitive together. If we *only* have a conjugated verb (*llevo*), the pronoun *must* be placed directly before the verb. If we *only* have an infinitive (*llevar*), the pronoun *must* be attached to the end of the verb.

Remember: when the subject and object of a sentence/phrase are the same person, the verb is considered *reflexive*. This means that the subject does an action to itself, for itself, etc.

Los pronombres reflexivos – Reflexive Pronouns

me – myself	**nos** – ourselves
te – yourself	**os** – yourselves (Spain plural)
se – himself / herself / yourself (formal)	**se** – themselves / yourselves (Latin America plural, formal)

A reflexive verb looks like any other verb, whether regular or irregular in any given verb tense, with the exception of the reflexive pronoun that accompanies it. It is this pronoun that makes the verb reflexive.

¡Ojo! The reflexive pronoun must match the subject in person (1st, 2nd, 3rd) and number (s., pl.).

Combinar dos complementos – Combining Two Objects

Mastering the sentence structure of Spanish is a difficult task, especially where object pronouns are concerned, so when you combine two objects in the same sentence, it becomes even more difficult. Take a look at the following examples of combined objects.

> *Ej.* ¿Te probaste el suéter en la tienda?   Did you try on the sweater at the store?
> Sí, me lo probé antes de comprarlo.   Yes, I tried it on before buying it.

In the above example, we have the reflexive verb *probarse* combined with the direct object *el suéter,* which is both masculine and singular. The direct object is then replaced with the corresponding pronoun: *lo* (masculine, singular).

> *Ej.* ¿Se ponen la ropa en el baño?   Do you put your clothing on in the bathroom?
> No, nos la ponemos en el dormitorio.   No, we put it on in the bedroom.

Whether you have only one object pronoun or are combining two, the placement rules still apply: immediately before a conjugated verb (*me lo* pongo) or attached to the end of an infinitive (ponér*melo*), but you must also place them in the proper order with respect to each other. If you are not sure which order to put them in, don't stress out; "ME LO" out. That is to say that the reflexive pronoun goes first and the direct-object pronoun goes second (*nos la, te los,* etc.).

Los verbos irregulares (el pretérito) – Irregular Verbs (preterite/past tense)

poner – to put		dar – to give		traer – to bring	
puse	pusimos	di	dimos	traje	trajimos
pusiste	pusisteis	diste	disteis	trajiste	trajisteis
puso	pusieron	dio	dieron	trajo	trajeron

Los comparativos – Comparatives

Comparatives, you may remember (p.18), make comparisons between two nouns. They can be used with adjectives, but the adjectives cannot always agree in gender and number with both nouns. This means that we have to treat the first part of the phrase as though it were the entire phrase, and then tack on the second noun afterward.

> *Ej.* La corbata es *más* barat<u>a</u>.   El chaleco es *menos* bonit<u>o</u>.
> La corbata es *más* barat<u>a</u> *que* el chaleco. El chaleco es *menos* bonit<u>o</u> *que* la corbata.
>
> Los anillos son *tan* car<u>os</u> *como* la blusa. (The rings are *as* expensive *as* the blouse.)
> La blusa es *tan* car<u>a</u> *como* los anillos. (The blouse is *as* expensive *as* the rings.)

- **Common comparative pitfall**

The phrase "more than" is not always a comparative. If you are talking about money and you say you have *more than* your friend, it's a comparative (comparison between you and your friend), but if you are saying you have *more than* $100 in your wallet, you are not comparing what you have to what $100 have, therefore it is not a comparative. This "than" is translated as *de*, not *que*. Think of it as "more *of* the same units." More than $100 is $101 (same units); it's not "I have."

> *Ej.* Tengo *más de* $100 en mi cartera.
> La blusa cuesta *menos de* $20.
> Hay *más de* 40 estudiantes en la clase.

La sustantivación de adjetivos – The Nominalization (Noun-ing) of Adjectives

Using direct-object pronouns is not the only way to avoid repetition of a noun. We can also turn adjectives into nouns. Consider the following phrases.

> "Which skirt do you prefer: the tight skirt or the loose skirt?"

Skirt, skirt, skirt. How many times do we need to say "skirt"? Exactly once, using "one" instead.

> "Which skirt do you prefer: the tight one or the loose one?"

In Spanish, this is accomplished by eliminating the noun, but leaving the article (*el, la,* etc.).

> *Ej.* ¿Qué falda prefieres: la ~~falda~~ apretada o la ~~falda~~ floja?
> Prefiero la ~~falda~~ apretada. (I prefer the tight one.)
> La ~~falda~~ que prefiero es la ~~falda~~ apretada. (The one I prefer is the tight one.)
>
> ¿Te gusta más el chaleco de rayas o el ~~chaleco~~ de cuadros?
> Me gusta más el de cuadros. (I prefer the plaid one.)
>
> ¿Cuál vestido es más elegante: el flojo y floreado o el corto y negro?
> Creo que el corto y negro es más elegante.

Unidad 15

We have covered the concept of subject-verb agreement unit after unit, and we have also covered the concept of indirect-object (pp.11, 24) and direct-object pronouns (pp.19, 22, 39-40). Independently, they are fairly basic concepts and are easily understood, but the sentence structure of Spanish creates problems for students when object pronouns are used.

¡*Ojo!* The most important thing to remember is that verbs can only be conjugated to subjects, never to objects. The subject does the action, the object receives the benefit or consequence of the action or is otherwise impacted by it.

Los pronombres de complemento indirecto – Indirect-Object Pronouns

me – me	**nos** – us
te – you	**os** – you (Spain plural)
le – him / her / you (formal)	**les** – them / you (Latin America plural, formal)

The best way to understand the use of indirect objects is to think of them as answering the questions: "*to whom?*" or "*for whom?*"

> *Ej.* Yo <u>le</u> pedí <u>al mesero</u> una ensalada. – I asked <u>the waiter</u> for a salad.
> Yo <u>le</u> pedí una ensalada. – I asked <u>him</u> for a salad.

In English, pronouns always replace nouns. In Spanish, in contrast, although they may replace nouns, they also may accompany them. In the case of indirect-object pronouns, it is most common to use the pronoun whether or not you use the noun, as you can see in the examples above.

There are two reasons to use the noun even when you use an indirect-object pronoun:

> ➢ to clarify the pronoun (*le, nos, os, les*)
> *Ej.* Mi mamá <u>nos</u> sirve la cena <u>a mí y a mi hermano</u>.

> ➢ to add emphasis
> *Ej.* <u>A ti</u> te gusta, pero <u>a mí</u> no (me gusta). – *You* like it, but *I* don't (like it).

In the case of *me* and *te*, there is never a need to clarify, but there may be a need to add emphasis. In English, we simply change our intonation to show that emphasis.

- **Common subject/object pitfall**

Be sure to keep your subject/object pronouns straight when concurring with someone.

> *Ej.* Juan – "<u>Me</u> gustan los tacos." ("Tacos please <u>me</u>.")
> María – "<u>Yo</u>, también." ("*I* also please you.") Are you sure that's what you mean?
> – "<u>A mí</u>, también." ("They also please <u>me</u>.") Now you're talking.

Los pronombres de complemento directo – Direct-Object Pronouns

lo – it (masculine)	**la** – it (feminine)
los – them (masculine / masculine and feminine)	**las** – them (feminine)

We have already studied direct-object pronouns (pp.19, 22, 39-40), so let's review.

> *Ej.* Did you already <u>order</u> **the enchiladas**?
> Yes, I <u>ordered</u> **them** already.
>
> ¿Ya <u>pediste</u> **las enchiladas**?
> Sí, ya **las** <u>pedí</u>.

Notice that *las enchiladas* is a feminine, plural noun and therefore it is replaced with the feminine, plural pronoun: *las*.

Combinar dos complementos – Combining Two Objects

Let's review the concept of combining two objects in the same sentence. Last unit, we combined direct-object pronouns with reflexive pronouns. This unit we will combine direct-object pronouns with indirect-object pronouns. Oh, yeah, and don't forget to "ME LO" out!

> *Ej.* ¿<u>Te</u> sirvió el mesero tu <u>sopa</u>?   Did the waiter serve <u>you</u> your <u>soup</u>?
> Sí, <u>me</u> <u>la</u> sirvió.   Yes, he served <u>it</u> <u>to me</u>.
>
> ¿<u>Me</u> va a traer mi <u>ensalada</u>?   Is she going to bring <u>me</u> my <u>salad</u>?
> Sí, <u>te</u> <u>la</u> va a traer ahora mismo.   Yes, she's going to bring <u>it</u> <u>to you</u> right now.
>   or
> ¿Va a traer<u>me</u> mi <u>ensalada</u>?
> Sí, va a traér<u>tela</u> ahora mismo

When the indirect-object pronouns *le* or *les* are combined with the direct-object pronouns *lo / la* or *los / las*, the *le* or *les* must be changed to *se*. This is to avoid the alliteration (repetition of a consonant sound), not because it is reflexive.

> *Ej.* ¿<u>Le</u> pediste <u>los tenedores</u>?   Did you ask <u>her</u> for <u>forks</u>?
> Sí, ~~le los~~ <u>se</u> <u>los</u> pedí hace 5 minutos.   Yes, I asked <u>her</u> for <u>them</u> 5 minutes ago.

Whether you have only one object pronoun or are combining two, the placement rules still apply: immediately before a conjugated verb (*me lo* sirvió) or attached to the end of an infinitive (servír*melo*). If you are still confused about which pronoun to put first, you may prefer the acronym R.I.D. (reflexive, indirect, direct). Apply it and *rid* yourself of the confusion.

Unidad 16

Los verbos irregulares (el presente y el pretérito) – Irregular Verbs (present and preterite)

In this unit, we will compare and contrast the present-tense conjugations with the preterite-tense conjugations of several irregular verbs. Remember that "irregular" is tense specific, which means that irregular in one tense does not mean irregular in another tense. Compare and contrast the following irregular verbs in the present and preterite.

presente   **pretérito**

perder (e → ie) – to lose   **perder**

pierdo	perdemos	perdí	perdimos
pierdes	perdéis	perdiste	perdisteis
pierde	pierden	perdió	perdieron

divertirse (e → ie) – to have fun   **divertirse (e → i)**

me divierto	nos divertimos	me divertí	nos divertimos
te diviertes	os divertís	te divertiste	os divertisteis
se divierte	se divierten	se divirtió	se divirtieron

Remember that stem-changing verbs in the present tense follow the basic guidelines below in the preterite. As you know, there are exceptions to almost every rule.

➢ **-ar** → regular

➢ **-er** → regular

➢ **-ir** → irregular, usually stem-changing in the 3rd person

The following irregular verbs require a change to maintain the pronunciation of certain consonants. This change is required in the 1st person, singular form (*yo*) in the preterite due to the *e* ending. These changes apply to all *-gar*, *-car*, and *-zar* verbs. For further review of this pronunciation issue, see pages 33-34.

jugar – to play (games)	**tocar – to play (instruments)**	**empezar – to begin**
yo jugué	yo toqué	yo empecé
tú jugaste	tú tocaste	tú empezaste

pagar – to pay (for)	**sacar – to take out**	**almorzar – to eat**
yo pagué	yo saqué	yo almorcé
tú pagaste	tú sacaste	tú almorzaste

colgar – to hang (up)	**masticar – to chew**	**lanzar – to throw**
yo colgué	yo mastiqué	yo lancé
tú colgaste	tú masticaste	tú lanzaste

Here is a review of the verbs *ser*, *ir* and *ver*. Remember that *ser* and *ir* have the same conjugations in the preterite tense but their meanings remain different. They can be distinguished only by context.

presente   **pretérito**

ir – to go

voy	vamos	fui	fuimos
vas	vais	fuiste	fuisteis
va	van	fue	fueron

ser – to be

soy	somos	fui	fuimos
eres	sois	fuiste	fuisteis
es	son	fue	fueron

ver – to see

veo	vemos	vi	vimos
ves	veis	viste	visteis
ve	ven	vio	vieron

¡Ojo! The *vosotros* forms in the present, and the *yo,* and *él/ella/Ud.* forms in the preterite are monosyllabic (one syllable) and therefore are too short to require an accent mark.

There are many preterite verbs that have an irregular stem change as well as irregular endings. The good thing is that almost all of them have the same irregular endings. You've already seen some of them, but here are the most common verbs that share these irregular endings.

presente   **pretérito**

hacer – to do / to make   hacer (hic/z)

hago	hacemos	**hice**	**hicimos**
haces	hacéis	**hiciste**	**hicisteis**
hace	hacen	**hizo**	**hicieron**

estar – to be   estar (estuv)

estoy	estamos	**estuve**	**estuvimos**
estás	estáis	**estuviste**	**estuvisteis**
está	están	**estuvo**	**estuvieron**

poder (o → ue) – to be able   poder (pud)

puedo	podemos	**pude**	**pudimos**
puedes	podéis	**pudiste**	**pudisteis**
puede	pueden	**pudo**	**pudieron**

¡Ojo! These irregular verbs in the preterite tense do not have accent marks.

presente		pretérito	

poner – to put / to place / to set **poner (pus)**

pongo	ponemos	pus<u>e</u>	pus<u>imos</u>
pones	ponéis	pus<u>iste</u>	pus<u>isteis</u>
pone	ponen	pus<u>o</u>	pus<u>ieron</u>

querer (e → ie) – to want **querer (quis)**

quiero	queremos	quis<u>e</u>	quis<u>imos</u>
quieres	queréis	quis<u>iste</u>	quis<u>isteis</u>
quiere	quieren	quis<u>o</u>	quis<u>ieron</u>

saber – to know (information) **saber (sup)**

sé	sabemos	sup<u>e</u>	sup<u>imos</u>
sabes	sabéis	sup<u>iste</u>	sup<u>isteis</u>
sabe	saben	sup<u>o</u>	sup<u>ieron</u>

tener (e → ie) – to have **tener (tuv)**

tengo	tenemos	tuv<u>e</u>	tuv<u>imos</u>
tienes	tenéis	tuv<u>iste</u>	tuv<u>isteis</u>
tiene	tienen	tuv<u>o</u>	tuv<u>ieron</u>

venir (e → ie) – to come **venir (vin)**

vengo	venimos	vin<u>e</u>	vin<u>imos</u>
vienes	venís	vin<u>iste</u>	vin<u>isteis</u>
viene	vienen	vin<u>o</u>	vin<u>ieron</u>

Verbs whose irregular stems end in *j* have a modification in the 3rd person, plural form.

decir (e → i) – to say / to tell **decir (dij)**

digo	decimos	dij<u>e</u>	dij<u>imos</u>
dices	decís	dij<u>iste</u>	dij<u>isteis</u>
dice	dicen	dij<u>o</u>	dij<u>eron</u> (no *i*)

traer – to bring **traer (traj)**

traigo	traemos	traj<u>e</u>	traj<u>imos</u>
traes	traéis	traj<u>iste</u>	traj<u>isteis</u>
trae	traen	traj<u>o</u>	traj<u>eron</u> (no *i*)

These irregular preterite verbs above are also irregular in the present in some way or another. Below is a very useful and unique verb: *dar*. Notice the similarities between *dar* and *ir* in the present and *dar* and *ver* in the preterite.

dar – to give (like *ir*) **dar** (like *ver*)

doy	damos	di	dimos
das	dais	diste	disteis
da	dan	dio	dieron

El presente progresivo – Progressive Present

You have learned that the main use of the present tense is to describe habitual action, and words like *siempre, nunca, todos los días, de vez en cuando,* etc. describe the frequency of that action. This, however, is not the only use of the present tense. The present tense can also be used to describe ongoing action that is taking place in the moment (right now).

> *Ej.* ¿Adónde vas (ahora)? – Where are you going (now)?
> Voy a la escuela (ahora). – I am going to school (now).

This use of the present could, in certain circumstances, be confused with habitual action. Although non-verbal cues (a person opening a door about to leave the house) or the word *ahora* would clarify the above conversation, without those non-verbal cues or clarifying words, it could be interpreted as habitual action.

> *Ej.* ¿Adónde vas (cada mañana)? – Where do you go (every morning)?
> Voy a la escuela (cada mañana). – I go to school (every morning).

To clarify this possible confusion, a modification of the present tense could be used: the progressive present. You've seen it before (p.20). This construction has two components: the verb *estar*, conjugated in the present tense, and the gerund form (-ing) of the action verb.

> *Ej.* ¿Qué **están** hac<u>iendo</u>? – What **are you (all)** do<u>ing</u>?
> **Estamos** desayun<u>ando</u>. – **We are** eat<u>ing</u> breakfast.

Review the verb *estar* in the present tense and notice the construction of the gerund (-ing).

estar – to be		-ing
estoy	estamos	-ar → -ando
estás	estáis	-er → -iendo
está	están	-ir → -iendo

¡Ojo! The verb *estar* is conjugated in the present tense according to the subject of the action. The action verb in the gerund (-ing) is not conjugated; it is an adverb, which has no subject or gender.

> *Ej.* **Estoy** com<u>iendo</u>. – **I am** eat<u>ing</u>.
> **Estás** com<u>iendo</u>. – **You are** eat<u>ing</u>.

There are irregular forms, and the changes are the same as the changes in stem-changing verbs in the preterite (3rd person). This means that *-ir* verbs are mainly affected.

> *Ej.* d<u>o</u>rmir (o → ue) – present   **d<u>o</u>rmir (o → u) – preterite**
> Mi hermano d<u>u</u>rmió mucho anoche. – My brother slept a lot last night.
> Mi hermano está d<u>u</u>rmiendo ahora. – My brother is sleeping right now.

Some verbs have an irregular gerund to break up the vowel sounds, whereas others, just because.

> *Ej.* le<u>y</u>endo ~~leiendo~~ (leer), tra<u>y</u>endo ~~traiendo~~ (traer), <u>y</u>endo ~~iendo~~ (ir), p<u>u</u>diendo (poder)

Unidad 17

Los verbos regulares (el imperfecto) – Regular Verbs (imperfect tense)

In this unit, we will focus on habitual action, which, as you know, cannot be represented by the preterite tense. So far, that has left the present tense as its sole representative. Now you will be introduced to the other past tense in Spanish – the imperfect tense. The imperfect tense is used to describe habitual action in the past (things that you used to do). There are other uses of the imperfect tense (p.80), but habitual action will be our focus here. As with the preterite, there are only two categories of verb endings: *-ar* and *-er/-ir*. Take a look at the following regular verbs in the imperfect tense.

jug<u>ar</u> – to play		corr<u>er</u> – to run	
jug<u>aba</u>	jug<u>ábamos</u>	corr<u>ía</u>	corr<u>íamos</u>
jug<u>abas</u>	jug<u>abais</u>	corr<u>ías</u>	corr<u>íais</u>
jug<u>aba</u>	jug<u>aban</u>	corr<u>ía</u>	corr<u>ían</u>

escrib<u>ir</u> – to write	
escrib<u>ía</u>	escrib<u>íamos</u>
escrib<u>ías</u>	escrib<u>íais</u>
escrib<u>ía</u>	escrib<u>ían</u>

¡Ojo! The *yo* and *él/ella/Ud.* forms are always the same as each other in the imperfect tense, so it's much more important that you use subject pronouns to maintain clarity.

> *Ej.* <u>Él</u> escribía muchas cartas de niño.
> <u>Yo</u> escribía muchas cartas de niño.

¡Ojo! Regular *-ar* verbs in the imperfect have an accent mark on the first *a* in the *nosotros* form.
Regular *-er* and *-ir* verbs in the imperfect all have accent marks on the first *i*.

The following is a review of some key words/phrases that signal habitual or routine action (whether present or past) and describe its frequency:

(casi) siempre – (almost) always	de vez en cuando – from time to time
(casi) nunca – (almost) never	por lo general – in general
(casi) todos los días – (almost) every day	generalmente – generally
cada semana – each week	normalmente – normally
a menudo – often	típicamente – typically
muchas veces – many times	frecuentemente – frequently
a veces – sometimes	constantemente – constantly
raras veces – rarely	

Los verbos irregulares (el imperfecto) – Irregular Verbs (imperfect tense)

You have already been introduced to regular imperfect-tense verbs. As you know, there are two parts to every verb in Spanish: the stem and the ending. By definition, all regular verbs retain the stem of their infinitives and only their endings change.

hablar	comer	vivir
hablaba	comía	vivía
hablabas	comías	vivías
hablaba	comía	vivía
hablábamos	comíamos	vivíamos
hablabais	comíais	vivíais
hablaban	comían	vivían

As with all verb tenses in Spanish, there are regular verbs and there are irregular verbs. The present and preterite tenses have countless irregular verbs, but in the imperfect tense, you can literally count the number of irregular verbs on one hand – three (*ser, ir, ver*). Take a look at these irregular verbs in both the present and imperfect tenses.

presente   **imperfecto**

	ser – to be			**ser**	
soy	somos		era	éramos
eres	sois		eras	erais
es	son		era	eran

	ir – to go			**ir**	
voy	vamos		iba	íbamos
vas	vais		ibas	ibais
va	van		iba	iban

	ver – to see / to watch			**ver**	
veo	vemos		veía	veíamos
ves	veis		veías	veíais
ve	ven		veía	veían

¡Ojo! The **NOSOTROS** form in the **IMPERFECT ALWAYS** has an **ACCENT MARK** whether the verb is regular, irregular, *-ar*, *-er*, or *-ir*.

Unidad 18

Los acentos escritos – Written Accent Marks

We have discussed accent marks throughout this course and they may still seem confusing and arbitrary, but when it comes to conjugating verbs, there are a few simple rules to remember and all of your accent-mark woes will be a thing of the past.

- The **present** tense: the *vosotros* form **almost always** has an accent mark.

  ➢ If the verb is an *-ar* verb, the accent mark goes over the *a*. hab<u>lar</u> → habl<u>áis</u>
  If the verb is an *-er* verb, the accent mark goes over the *e*. com<u>er</u> → com<u>éis</u>
  If the verb is an *-ir* verb, the accent mark goes over the *i*. viv<u>ir</u> → viv<u>ís</u>

  The exceptions are conjugations that are monosyllabic (one syllable): *sois, vais, veis, dais,* etc.

- The **preterite** tense: the *yo* and the *él/ella/Ud.* forms **normally** have an accent mark on the last letter of the ending.

  ➢ hab<u>lé</u>   com<u>í</u>   viv<u>í</u>
  hab<u>laste</u>   com<u>iste</u>   viv<u>iste</u>
  hab<u>ló</u>   com<u>ió</u>   viv<u>ió</u>

  The exceptions are conjugations that are monosyllabic: *fui, fue, vi, vio, di, dio,* etc. and conjugations with irregular endings: *tuve, puse, traje, estuvo, quiso, dijo, supo,* etc.

  ➢ Irregular verbs that have regular endings still have accent marks:
  jugué, toqué, comencé, etc.

- The **imperfect** tense: **all six conjugations forms** of *-er,* and *-ir* verbs **almost always** have an accent mark on the first *i* of the ending.

  ➢ com<u>ía</u>   com<u>íamos</u>   viv<u>ía</u>   viv<u>íamos</u>
  com<u>ías</u>   com<u>íais</u>   viv<u>ías</u>   viv<u>íais</u>
  com<u>ía</u>   com<u>ían</u>   viv<u>ía</u>   viv<u>ían</u>

  The exceptions are the irregular verbs with irregular endings: *ser, ir.*

  The *nosotros* form **always** has an accent mark on the first letter of the ending.

  ➢ hab<u>lábamos</u>, com<u>íamos</u>, viv<u>íamos</u>, ve<u>íamos</u>, <u>éramos</u>, <u>íbamos</u>

We have covered the concept of subject-verb agreement unit after unit since the beginning, and we have also covered the concept of indirect-object (pp.11, 24, 42-43), direct-object (pp.19, 22, 39-40, 43), and reflexive pronouns (pp.25-27, 36-38). Independently, they are fairly basic concepts and are easily understood, but the sentence structure of Spanish creates problems for students when object pronouns are used.

¡Ojo! **The most important thing to remember is that verbs can only be conjugated to subjects, never to objects. The subject does the action, the object receives the benefit or consequence of the action or is otherwise impacted by it.**

Los pronombres de complemento indirecto – Indirect-Object Pronouns

me – me	**nos** – us
te – you	**os** – you (Spain plural)
le – him / her / you (formal)	**les** – them / you (Latin America plural, formal)

The best way to understand the use of indirect objects is to think of them as answering the following questions: *"to whom?"* or *"for whom?"*

> *Ej.* Yo le di un regalo a mi hermano. – I gave a gift to my brother.
> Yo le di un regalo. – I gave a gift to him.

In English, pronouns always replace nouns. In Spanish, in contrast, although they may replace nouns, they also often accompany them. In the case of indirect-object pronouns, it is most common to use the pronoun whether you use the noun or not. A general guideline is that you can sometimes leave out the pronoun if the noun is 3rd person, but not for 1st or 2nd person nouns. If you always use the indirect-object pronouns, regardless of person, you can never go wrong.

There are two reasons to use the noun even when you use an indirect-object pronoun:

> ➢ to clarify the pronoun (*le, nos, os, les*)
>   *Ej.* Mi mamá nos sirve la cena a mí y a mi hermano.
>   Yo les di $100 a mis hijos para la Navidad.

> ➢ to add emphasis
>   *Ej.* A ti te gusta, pero a mí no (me gusta). – *You* like it, but *I* don't (like it).

In the case of *me* and *te*, there is never a need to clarify, but there may be a need to add emphasis. In English, we simply change our intonation to show that emphasis.

¡Ojo! Indirect-object pronouns typically represent people or animals because they are capable of receiving the action or direct object, but sometimes they are used to represent inanimate objects.

> *Ej.* Le eché un poco de sal a la sopa.

Los pronombres de complemento directo – Direct-Object Pronouns

me – me	**nos** – us
te – you	**os** – you (Spain plural)
lo – him / it (masculine)	**los** – them (masculine / masculine and feminine)
la – her / it (feminine)	**las** – them (feminine)

In contrast to indirect objects almost always being animate (living), we have studied direct objects as inanimate (not living), but direct objects are as commonly animate as they are inanimate.

The best way to understand the use of direct objects is to think of them as answering the following questions: "*whom?*" or "*what?*"

> *Ej.* ¿Tienes tu <u>mochila</u> aquí?
> Sí, yo <u>la</u> tengo conmigo.

> Do you have your <u>backpack</u> here?
> Yes, I have <u>it</u> with me.

> ¿Abrazas a tu <u>abuela</u>?
> Sí, yo <u>la</u> abrazo cada vez que <u>la</u> veo.

> Do you hug your <u>grandma</u>?
> Yes, I hug <u>her</u> each time I see <u>her</u>.

In the examples above, it is easy to identify the backpack as a direct object because it answers the question "*what?*" but it is more difficult to identify the grandma as a direct object as opposed to an indirect object because it is a person. When trying to determine whether you need an indirect-object pronoun (*le, les*) or a direct-object pronoun (*lo / la, los / las*), ask yourself this:

> Do I hug *to* my grandma (*to* whom; indirect) or do I hug my grandma (whom; direct)?

This is not a perfect, fail-safe system, as not everything will translate perfectly to and from English, but it gives you a basic understanding of the difference between direct and indirect.

- **La "*a personal*" – The "personal *a*"**

This is a difficult concept to understand for students because it doesn't exist in most languages. Since the sentence structure of the Spanish language is so flexible, it would be much harder to distinguish the subject from the object in context without the "personal *a*." In English, the subject and object can be easily identified by their placement in the sentence.

> *Ej.* I love my dad. "I" (subject doing the loving) comes before the verb and "my dad" (object receiving the love) comes after the verb.

In Spanish, the subject or object can come first, leaving the reader/listener in need of other cues.

> *Ej.* Yo amo <u>a</u> mi papá. *Yo* (subject doing the loving) is not preceded by *a* whereas *mi papá* (object receiving the love) is preceded by *a*.

Although this *a* has no translation in English, it is required for direct objects that are people (optional with animals) but not before a direct-object pronoun (*me, te, lo / la, nos, os, los / las*).

When the subject and object (indirect or direct) of a sentence/phrase are the same person, the verb is considered *reflexive*. This means that the subject does an action to itself, for itself, etc.

Los pronombres reflexivos – Reflexive Pronouns

me – myself	**nos** – ourselves
te – yourself	**os** – yourselves (Spain plural)
se – himself / herself / yourself (formal)	**se** – themselves / yourselves (Latin America plural, formal)

A reflexive verb looks like any other verb, whether regular or irregular in any given verb tense, with the exception of the reflexive pronoun that accompanies it. It is this pronoun that makes the verb reflexive.

¡Ojo! The reflexive pronoun must match the subject in person (1ˢᵗ, 2ⁿᵈ, 3ʳᵈ) and number (s., pl.).

Combinar dos complementos – Combining Two Objects

Mastering the sentence structure of Spanish is a difficult task, especially where object pronouns are concerned, so when you combine two objects in the same sentence, it becomes even more difficult. Take a look at the following examples of combined objects.

> *Ej.* ¿Quién <u>te</u> regaló esa <u>computadora</u>? Who gave <u>you</u> that <u>computer</u>?
> Mi mamá <u>me la</u> regaló. My mom gave <u>it to me</u>.

> ¿<u>Te</u> lavas el <u>pelo</u> cuando te bañas? Do you wash your <u>hair</u> when you bathe?
> Sí, <u>me lo</u> lavo cada vez que me baño. Yes, I wash <u>it</u> each time I bathe.

Notice that in the first example, there is an <u>indirect</u>-object pronoun combined with a <u>direct</u>-object pronoun, whereas in the second example, there is a <u>reflexive</u> pronoun combined with a <u>direct</u>-object pronoun. When the indirect-object pronouns *le* or *les* are combined with the direct-object pronouns *lo / la* or *los / las*, the *le* or *les* must be changed to *se*. This is to avoid the alliteration (repetition of a consonant sound), not because it is reflexive.

> *Ej.* ¿Quién <u>le</u> regaló esa <u>computadora</u>? Who gave <u>her</u> that <u>computer</u>?
> Mi mamá ~~le la~~ <u>se la</u> regaló. Mi mom gave <u>it to her</u>.

As you hopefully remember, object pronouns, whether direct, indirect, or reflexive, are placed separately before a conjugated verb (*me lo sirvió*) or attached to the end of an infinitive (*buscármelo*) or gerund form (*comprándomelo*) of the verb. If you are combining two object pronouns, the same rules apply but you must also place them in the proper order with respect to each other. If you are not sure which order to put them in, don't stress out; "ME LO" out. That is to say that the direct-object pronoun goes second whether the first one is reflexive or indirect. Or you may prefer the acronym R.I.D. (reflexive, indirect, direct) to *rid* yourself of the confusion.

Unidad 19

Los verbos que implican o indican el futuro – Verbs That Imply or Indicate the Future

There are many tenses in the Spanish language and you have been exposed to three distinct ones (present, preterite, and imperfect), not counting progressive forms, but you also learned early on (p.16) how to talk about the future without using the future tense. With the verb *ir* plus the preposition *a* followed by the infinitive of another verb, you can talk about things that *are going to happen*.

> *Ej.* <u>Voy a jugar</u> al béisbol el próximo sábado.
>
> Mis papás y yo <u>vamos a visitar</u> a mis abuelos este verano.

This is done with the present tense of the conjugated verb (*ir*). The assumption is that you are proceeding with the plans now, in the present, to do something in the future. Although you may have never thought of them in this way, you already know other verbs that serve the same function: *querer, preferir, tener que, necesitar, deber*, etc.

> *Ej.* Quiero (ahora) viajar (en el futuro) a México durante las vacaciones.
>
> Necesitamos (ahora) comprar (en el futuro) un boleto de ida y vuelta.

In the above examples, we see a need or a want that is current, even though the action to be carried out is in the future.

Los tiempos progresivos – Progressive Tenses

You've been working with the progressive present for a while now (pp.20, 47), but you can use the progressive form with any verb tense. You can say what someone *was* doing, *will be* doing, *has been* doing, *would be* doing, *would have been* doing, etc. All you need is the correct tense and conjugation of the verb *estar* and the very same gerund forms (*-ando, -iendo*) you already know. Don't forget about the irregular forms (p.47).

> *Ej.* **Estoy** jugando al fútbol ahora. (present – shows what's happening at *this* moment)
> **Estuve** jugando al fútbol por cuatro horas. (preterite – shows duration of time)
> **Estaba** jugando al fútbol cuando me llamaste. (imperfect – shows background info.,
> what was happening at *that* moment)
>
> **Estamos** leyendo su novela. (present – shows what's happening at *this* momento)
> **Estuvimos** leyendo su novela toda la noche. (preterite – shows duration of time)
> **Estábamos** leyendo cuando nos llamaste. (imperfect – shows background info.,
> what was happening at *that* moment)

Los mandatos / las órdenes (el imperativo) – Commands / Orders (imperative mood)

We have all been told what to do as well as told others what to do, so we are familiar with the concept of commands. How to conjugate them in Spanish is a different story. Let's take the following example for starters: your mom tells you, "Clean your room." What verb tense is the verb "clean"? Could she have meant, "Clean your room *last week*"? Of course not; a command cannot be given in the present for a past action. So, is it possibly present or near future? "Clean your room *right now / before I get home*"? Absolutely. So is this the present tense in Spanish? It would seem that commands are the present tense, but what happens if you tell your mom, "no," or you simply don't do it for any number of possible reasons? Does any *cleaning* end up getting done? As you can see, commands cannot be the present tense because it merely shows what someone *wants* to happen but it cannot be confirmed that the event actually takes place at the time indicated in the command. So, we can conclude that commands are similar to the present tense, but they are not identical.

The most important thing to remember about commands is that since we cannot confirm that an action will take place, much less *when* it will take place, they are not considered to be a verb tense (tense meaning time). This means that several rules we have learned so far are not valid with commands. We will cover these differences as we go.

This unit, as the concept of commands is quite new, we will focus on familiar, 2nd person commands (*tú*). There are two forms to understand: affirmative (do it) and negative (don't do it). And, as always, we must consider the ending of the verb in question.

comprar
affirmative (+) tú: compr<u>a</u> (buy)   negative (–) tú: <u>no</u> compr<u>es</u> (don't buy)

prender
affirmative (+) tú: prend<u>e</u> (turn on)   negative (–) tú: <u>no</u> prend<u>as</u> (don't turn on)

compartir
affirmative (+) tú: compart<u>e</u> (share)   negative (–) tú: <u>no</u> compart<u>as</u> (don't share)

The first thing to note is that the affirmative command looks like the *él / ella* form in the present (-*ar* → -*a*, -*er* → -*e*, -*ir* → -*e*). The second thing to note is that the negative command requires the opposite ending of the *tú* form in the present (-*ar* → -*es*, -*er* → -*as*, -*ir* → -*as*).

Los mandatos irregulares – Irregular Commands

Although commands are not a verb tense, there are still irregular conjugations. Commands cannot be in the past, and although they are not quite fully present because of the possibility that the desired action won't be carried out, irregularities in the present are what determine whether a command is regular or irregular.

All stem-changing verbs in the present maintain the same change in the command forms. Since *tú* has a change in the present, all stem-changing verbs will be irregular in the *tú* command form whether it is affirmative or negative.

mostrar (o → ue)

presente: muestro
muestras
muestra   muestran

mandato (+) tú: muestra
(–) tú: no muestres

volver (o → ue)

presente: vuelvo
vuelves
vuelve   vuelven

mandato (+) tú: vuelve
(–) tú: no vuelvas

conseguir (e → i)

presente: consigo
consigues
consigue   consiguen

mandato (+) tú: consigue
(–) tú: no consigas

As you know, stem-changing verbs are not the only irregular verbs in the present; sometimes the *yo* form has a unique ending. In these cases, the root of the command form looks like the root of either the infinitive (*tú*, affirmative commands) or the *yo* form (*tú*, negative commands).

salir →	salgo	affirmative (+) tú: sal	negative (–) tú: no salgas
tener →	tengo	affirmative (+) tú: ten	negative (–) tú: no tengas
poner →	pongo	affirmative (+) tú: pon	negative (–) tú: no pongas
traer →	traigo	affirmative (+) tú: trae	negative (–) tú: no traigas
hacer →	hago	affirmative (+) tú: haz	negative (–) tú: no hagas
ver →	veo	affirmative (+) tú: ve	negative (–) tú: no veas
ir →	voy	affirmative (+) tú: ve	negative (–) tú: no vayas

Los mandatos reflexivos – Reflexive Commands

Another thing that is different about commands is that the placement of object pronouns is determined by whether the command is affirmative or negative. Notice that the pronoun in the affirmative command is attached to the end, forming one word. This may create the need for an accent mark that is not needed in the negative form. We will discuss this accent more next unit.

abrocharse	affirmative (+) tú: abróchate	negative (–) tú: no te abroches
sentarse (e → ie)	affirmative (+) tú: siéntate	negative (–) tú: no te sientes

Unidad 20

Los mandatos / las órdenes (el imperativo) – Commands / Orders (imperative mood)

You are now familiar with the concept of commands and the differences between their conjugation rules and the conjugation rules for verb tenses. But so far, you have only seen the *tú* forms. In reality, there are commands for 1ˢᵗ and 2ⁿᵈ person forms except for the *yo* form. If you found yourself giving yourself a command, you would probably use the *tú* form, unless of course you were worried about offending yourself; then you would obviously use the more formal *Ud.* form. And if you are talking to yourself, anything is possible. For *nosotros* and *vosotros* command forms, see pages 109-110.

¡Ojo! You must be talking *to* someone to give him or her a command, therefore there are no commands for 3ʳᵈ person (*él / ella, ellos / ellas*), which are used to talk *about* someone.

In this unit, we will expand on what you already know by incorporating the *Ud.* and *Uds.* forms. Just as with any verb conjugation, the *tú* form is used in familiar settings (friends, family, children, etc.), whereas *Ud.* is used in formal settings (adults that you don't know very well). *Uds.*, on the other hand, can be used as the plural form of *tú* or *Ud.* in Latin America.

As with the *tú* forms, irregulars in the present are irregulars in the command form. Take a look at the following verbs and notice the patterns.

apoyar

(+) tú: apoya
(–) tú: no apoyes

(+) Ud.: apoye   (+) Uds.: apoyen
(–) Ud.: no apoye   (–) Uds.: no apoyen

resolver (o → ue)

(+) tú: resuelve
(–) tú: no resuelvas

(+) Ud.: resuelva   (+) Uds.: resuelvan
(–) Ud.: no resuelva   (–) Uds.: no resuelvan

influir (y)

(+) tú: influye
(–) tú: no influyas

(+) Ud.: influya   (+) Uds.: influyan
(–) Ud.: no influya   (–) Uds.: no influyan

Notice that the *tú*, affirmative command is the *only* form here that maintains the present-tense endings; all others require the opposite ending of their respective present-tense conjugations.

Remember our list of irregulars where the *yo* form in the present had a unique conjugation (p.56)? Their patterns are similar to other commands when it comes to the *Ud.* and *Uds.* forms.

<u>sal</u>ir → <u>sal</u>go	(+) tú: <u>sal</u>	(–) tú: no <u>sal</u>gas	(+/–) Ud.: <u>sal</u>ga	(+/–) Uds.: <u>sal</u>gan
<u>ten</u>er → <u>ten</u>go	(+) tú: <u>ten</u>	(–) tú: no <u>ten</u>gas	(+/–) Ud.: <u>ten</u>ga	(+/–) Uds.: <u>ten</u>gan
<u>pon</u>er → <u>pon</u>go	(+) tú: <u>pon</u>	(–) tú: no <u>pon</u>gas	(+/–) Ud.: <u>pon</u>ga	(+/–) Uds.: <u>pon</u>gan
<u>tra</u>er → <u>tra</u>igo	(+) tú: <u>tra</u>e	(–) tú: no <u>tra</u>igas	(+/–) Ud.: <u>tra</u>iga	(+/–) Uds.: <u>tra</u>igan
<u>hac</u>er → <u>hag</u>o	(+) tú: <u>haz</u>	(–) tú: no <u>hag</u>as	(+/–) Ud.: <u>hag</u>a	(+/–) Uds.: <u>hag</u>an
ver → <u>ve</u>o	(+) tú: <u>ve</u>	(–) tú: no <u>ve</u>as	(+/–) Ud.: <u>ve</u>a	(+/–) Uds.: <u>ve</u>an
ir → voy	(+) tú: ve	(–) tú: no <u>va</u>yas	(+/–) Ud.: <u>va</u>ya	(+/–) Uds.: <u>va</u>yan
<u>ven</u>ir → <u>ven</u>go	(+) tú: <u>ven</u>	(–) tú: no <u>ven</u>gas	(+/–) Ud.: <u>ven</u>ga	(+/–) Uds.: <u>ven</u>gan
decir → <u>dig</u>o	(+) tú: di	(–) tú: no <u>dig</u>as	(+/–) Ud.: <u>dig</u>a	(+/–) Uds.: <u>dig</u>an
<u>ser</u> → soy	(+) tú: sé	(–) tú: no <u>se</u>as	(+/–) Ud.: <u>se</u>a	(+/–) Uds.: <u>se</u>an
<u>dar</u> → doy	(+) tú: da	(–) tú: no des	(+/–) Ud.: dé	(+/–) Uds.: den

Remember *abrocharse* and *sentarse* from last unit? They were the two examples of reflexive verbs in command form I gave you. This unit, we will study many reflexive verbs and we will add in the *Ud.* and *Uds.* forms. Notice the difference in reflexive pronouns as well as their placement.

quejar<u>se</u>

(+) tú: quéja<u>te</u>
(–) tú: <u>no te</u> quejes

(+) Ud.: quéje<u>se</u>	**(+) Uds.:** quéjen<u>se</u>
(–) Ud.: <u>no se</u> queje	**(–) Uds.:** <u>no se</u> quejen

reír<u>se</u> (e → í)

(+) tú: ríe<u>te</u>
(–) tú: <u>no te</u> rías

(+) Ud.: ría<u>se</u>	**(+) Uds.:** rían<u>se</u>
(–) Ud.: <u>no se</u> ría	**(–) Uds.:** <u>no se</u> rían

All object pronouns (*me, te, se, le, lo / la, nos, os, se, les, los / las*) follow the same rules within a given conjugation form whether that is a verb tense or a command.

explicar

(+) tú: explíca<u>me</u>
(–) tú: <u>no me</u> expliques

(+) Ud.: explíque<u>lo</u>	**(+) Uds.:** explíquen<u>melo</u>
(–) Ud.: <u>no lo</u> explique	**(–) Uds.:** <u>no me lo</u> expliquen

Los acentos escritos – Written Accent Marks

You should now be aware of the importance of written accent marks, especially with verb conjugations (p.50), but you still do not know how to use them in every circumstance to maintain proper pronunciation. To better understand them, take a look at these basic rules:

➤ If the word ends in a vowel (*a, e, i, o, u*), *n* or *s*, the normal, unaccented stress falls on the second-to-last (penultimate) syllable.

ha·bl<u>o</u>	ha·bla·mo<u>s</u>	co·m<u>o</u>	co·me·mo<u>s</u>
ha·bla<u>s</u>		co·me<u>s</u>	
ha·bl<u>a</u>	ha·bla<u>n</u>	co·m<u>e</u>	co·me<u>n</u>

➤ If the word ends in a consonant other than *n* or *s*, the normal, unaccented stress falls on the last syllable.

ha·bl<u>ar</u>   co·m<u>er</u>   vi·v<u>ir</u>

➤ If the word does not follow the above rules, a written accent must be used to show where the proper stress falls.

ha·blá<u>is</u>   co·mé<u>is</u>   ha·bl<u>ó</u>   co·m<u>í</u>   ha·blá·ba·mo<u>s</u>

You've learned *where* accent marks are required in the present, preterite and imperfect tenses (p.50), and now you know *why*.

Only by understanding *why* we need written accent marks can we possibly know *where* to put them since it is impossible to memorize every single word in the Spanish language. Last unit, I pointed out that affirmative reflexive commands have written accent marks, but negative reflexive commands do not. Applying the rules above, we should now be able to understand why.

a·bro·ch<u>a</u>   a·bró·cha·t<u>e</u>   no te a·bro·che<u>s</u>

The stressed syllable in the above examples is *bro*. The first and third examples follow the first rule (second-to-last syllable stressed), whereas the second example followed the third rule (breaking the first rule). By attaching the pronoun *te* to the end of the word *abrocha*, we added a syllable. This would have changed the second-to-last syllable from *bro* to *cha*. In order to avoid this change and maintain the original stress, a written accent is required.

This accent mark is also required with infinitives and gerund forms when we attach a pronoun to the end. Take a look at the following examples and see if you can identify why some have accent marks and others do not.

comprar	lavar	regalando
comprarlo	lavarse	regalándolo
comprármelo	lavárselas	regalándonoslo

Los comparativos – Comparatives

Comparatives, you may remember (pp.18, 41), make comparisons between two nouns. You know they can be used with adjectives and adverbs, but they can also be used with verbs. In the case of verbs, the issue of which subject the verb is conjugated to arises, but easy enough, the solution is the same as it is for adjectives: you simply conjugate according to the first noun.

> *Ej.* Pablito grita *más*.   Mis hermanos gritan *más*.
> Pablito grita *más que* mis hermanos.   Mis hermanos gritan *más que* Pablito.
>
> Pablito grita *tanto como* mis hermanos. (Pablito shouts *as much as* my brothers do.)

Although, in English, we often confuse object pronouns (me, him, us, them, etc.) with subject pronouns (I, he, we, they, etc.), they are never confused by native speakers in Spanish. If you are comparing subjects in Spanish, use subject pronouns across the board. If you are comparing objects (direct or indirect), use object pronouns across the board.

> *Ej.* Verenice da *mejores* consejos *que* yo. (… *mejores* consejos *que* ~~mí~~.)
> Yo doy *mejores* consejos *que* Verenice.
>
> Magda te respeta a ti *más que* a mí.
> Yo te respeto a ti *más que* a Magda. (Notice the "personal *a*.")

What happens when we confuse our pronouns?

> *Ej.* Magda te respeta a ti *más que* a mí. (Magda respects you *more than* she respects me.)
> Magda te respeta a ti *más que* yo. (Magda respects you *more than* I respect you.)
>
> A ti te gusta correr *más que* a mí. (You like running *more than* I like running.)
>   (Literally: running please you *more than* it pleases me.)
> A ti te gusta correr *más que* yo. (You like running *more than* you like me.)
>   (Literally: running pleases you *more than* I please you.)

With this in mind, let's see a different type of comparative: "My teacher treats me *like* a child."

> *Ej.* Mi maestra me trata *como* un niño. (My teacher treats me *like* a child would.)
> Mi maestra me trata *como* a un niño. (My teacher treats me *like* she would a child.)

The only difference is the "personal *a*," which tells us *un niño* is an object, not a subject.

- **Common comparative pitfall**

Do you remember the common comparative pitfall of *de* vs. *que* (p.41)? Consider the following phrase: "You are taller than I thought." Is this a comparative? Is this a comparison between how tall "you" are and how tall "I thought" is? Of course not; that doesn't even make sense.

> *Ej.* "*Eres más alto* **que** *yo pensé*." ??? Nope!
> "*Eres más alto* **de lo que** *yo pensé*." ??? Now you're speakin' my language!

60

Los superlativos – Superlatives

Superlatives are similar to comparatives in structure, but what makes nouns "super" is that there *is* no comparison, or in other words, everything else pales in comparison. Since there is no comparison, there is no question as to which noun the adjectives modify.

> *Ej.* Maribel es *la más* talentos<u>a</u>. (Maribel is *the most* talented.)
> Alejandro es *el más* talentos<u>o</u>. (Alejandro is *the most* talented.)

Without making a direct comparison with anyone in particular, you can give context if you wish.

> *Ej.* Brenda es *la menos* vanidos<u>a</u> (de toda la clase).
> Joel es *el menos* egoísta (de todos los estudiantes).

When asking a question about a group of females, the adjectives are feminine. When asking about a group of males or a mixed group of males and females, the adjectives are masculine. The gender (and number) of the answer is independent of the gender (and number) in the question.

> *Ej.* ¿Quién es *el más* comprensiv<u>o</u> de todos los pasajeros?
> Irene es *la más* comprensiv<u>a</u> de todos los pasajeros.

The plural forms look as you probably expect.

> *Ej.* ¿Quiénes son *los más* considerad<u>os</u>?
> Las señoras son *las más* considerad<u>as</u>.

- *el (más), la (más), lo (más)* **and the nominalization (noun-ing) of adjectives**

You've learned that you can turn an adjective into a noun by using the noun's article and the adjective in question (p.41). This is what is happening in the examples above. When referring to a masculine noun, use *el*/*los*. When referring to a feminine noun, use *la*/*las*. This is like saying "the one(s)." But if what you are referring to is unspecified or abstract, use what some people call the neuter form, *lo*, and the masculine form of the adjective. This is like saying "the thing."

> *Ej.* *lo que* me gusta (más) es – *what* I like (most) is / *the thing* that I like (most) is
> *lo* (más) *chistos<u>o</u>* es su pelo – *the funny*(est) *thing* is her hair
> *lo peor* es que – *the worst thing* is that

- **Common superlative pitfall**

Although *más* means "more" and "most," for expressions like "<u>The more</u> Spanish I learn, <u>the more</u> confidence I have," do not use *lo más*. Instead, use *cuanto/a(s) más*, *mientras más*, or *entre más* for the first part, and *más* or *mejor* for the second part. *Menos* and *peor* can work in some cases.

> *Ej.* *Cuant<u>o</u> más* español aprendo, *más* confianza tengo. (*cuanto* modifies *español*)
> *Cuant<u>as</u> más* clases de español tomo, *mejor* lo hablo. (*cuantas* modifies *clases*)
> *Mientras más* español aprendo, *más* confianza tengo.
> *Entre más* clases de español tomo, *mejor* lo hablo.

Unidad 21

El participio pasado – Past Participle

The past participle is not a difficult concept to understand, but due to differences in Spanish and English, many students struggle with it. In English, you might know of it as the "ed" form of a verb. The problem with that understanding is that the regulars in the past tense (preterite) and the regulars in the past participle both end in "ed."

> *Ej.* The door is <u>closed</u>. (past participle)
> I <u>closed</u> the door. (past tense)

In the first example, the word *closed* is a description of the state of the door. In the second example, we have a description of an action but know nothing of the state of the door because we don't know whether or not someone opened it afterward. When either the past tense or the past participle is irregular, we can clearly see the difference.

> *Ej.* My essay is <u>written</u>. (past participle)
> I <u>wrote</u> my essay. (past tense)

In the first example, we learn of the state of the essay. In the second, we know how it got that way. What we don't know in the second example is whether it is still that way. In both cases, we have irregular forms and these would rarely be confused by a native speaker of English.

El participio pasado como adjetivo – Past Participle as an Adjective.

In the examples above, the past participle was used as an adjective; it served as a description of a noun. In Spanish, it serves the same function. The difference between Spanish and English, however, is that adjectives in Spanish have gender (masculine and feminine) and number (singular and plural). In English, these concepts do not exist for adjectives.

> *Ej.* Mi <u>papá</u> está enoja<u>do</u>.
> Mi <u>mamá</u> está aburri<u>da</u>.
> Mis <u>papás</u> están divorci<u>ados</u>.

You have probably already used the above examples in context without knowing that these adjectives were past participles. The most important thing to understand is that the root of a past participle is a verb, but the past participle itself is not a verb; sometimes it is an adjective (modifying a noun), sometimes it is an adverb (modifying a verb).

> verb: cansar(se) → adjective: cansado/a
> divertir(se) → divertido/a

¡Ojo! Verbs can be reflexive, but adjectives cannot.

Since past participles come from verbs, in order to understand how to form them, we must know whether the verb is an *-ar*, *-er*, or *-ir* verb. Notice that *-er* and *-ir* verbs have the same endings.

-ar	**-er**	**-ir**
-ado, -ados, -ada, -adas	-ido, -idos, -ida, -idas	-ido, -idos, -ida, -idas

Adjectives are used most frequently with the verbs *estar*, *ser*, and *parecer*, and past participles are no exception.

> *Ej.* El aire <u>está</u> contaminado.
> La vida urbana <u>es</u> muy animada.
> El campo <u>parece</u> muy aburrido.

In English as well as in Spanish, there are irregular forms of the past participle, but being irregular in one language does not make it irregular in another language. In contrast to the regular endings, these ones (among others) in Spanish end in *to*, *ta*, *tos*, or *tas*.

abrir	→	abierto	to open	→	open (not opened)
escribir	→	escrito	to write	→	written (not writed)
inscribir(se)	→	inscrito	to sign up	→	signed up (regular)
describrir	→	descrito	to describe	→	described (regular)
poner(se)	→	puesto	to put (on)	→	on (not puted)
ver	→	visto	to see	→	seen (not seed)
resolver	→	resuelto	to resolve	→	resolved (regular)
volver	→	vuelto	to return	→	back (not returned)
morir(se)	→	muerto	to die	→	dead (not died)
freír	→	frito (also freído)	to fry	→	fried (not fryed)
romper	→	roto	to break	→	broken (not breaked)
			to tear	→	torn (not teared)

There are also a few that have a different irregular ending: *-cho*, *-cha*, *-chos*, or *-chas*

decir	→	dicho	to say	→	said (not sayed)
			to tell	→	told (not telled)
hacer	→	hecho	to do	→	done (not doed)
			to make	→	made (not maked)

You have seen a few of these irregulars without knowing that they were past participles of verbs.

> *Ej.* Mi bisabuela está <u>muerta</u>. (morir)
> Me gustan las papas <u>fritas</u>. (freír)
> La artesanía es <u>hecha</u> a mano. (hacer)

Los verbos (el presente perfecto) – Verbs (present-perfect tense)

You have already studied in depth the present, preterite, and imperfect tenses as well as commands (not a tense). Now you will see your fourth verb tense: the present perfect. The present-perfect tense, both in English and Spanish, is often interchangeable with the preterite tense; both describe past actions. The difference between the two is that the present perfect connects those past actions to the present, whereas the preterite does not. Consider the following examples in English.

> *Ej.* They <u>lived</u> in the city for 10 years. (They probably don't live there anymore.)
> They <u>have lived</u> in the city for 10 years. (They probably still live there.)

Take a look at some more examples of the present perfect in English.

> *Ej.* I <u>have walked</u> to school before.
> They <u>have written</u> six essays for that class.
> She <u>has done</u> her homework every day this year.

The present-perfect tense is called a *compound* tense because it has two components: a helping verb (to have) and the past participle of the verb you are conjugating. Above, you have a regular past participle (-ed), a common irregular (-en) and one that is completely irregular (done). In English, the helping verb is *to have*, but that is not the verb *tener* in Spanish. *Tener* is used to show possession, but in the case of the present perfect, we use the verb *haber* conjugated in the present tense followed by a past participle. The past participle here is an adverb (no gender or number).

haber – to have (not possession)   **-ed**

he	hemos		-ar → -ado (~~ados~~, ~~ada~~, ~~adas~~)
has	habéis		-er → -ido (~~idos~~, ~~ida~~, ~~idas~~)
ha	han		-ir → -ido (~~idos~~, ~~ida~~, ~~idas~~)

There are a few verbs, both in English and Spanish, where the form of the past participle changes depending on whether it is an adjective or part of the present-perfect tense. Take a look at a couple of examples in English.

> *Ej.* My grandfather is <u>dead</u>. (to die)   My grandfather has <u>died</u>. (to die)
> My brother is <u>asleep</u>. (to sleep)   My brother has <u>slept</u>. (to sleep)

Both of these examples would use the same word in Spanish:

> *Ej.* Mi abuelo está <u>muerto</u>. (morir)   Mi abuelo ha <u>muerto</u>. (morir)
> Mi hermano está <u>dormido</u>. (dormir)   Mi hermano ha <u>dormido</u>. (dormir)

Since this is an introduction to the concepts of past participles, let's focus on the verbs whose past participles are the same in adjective form as well as in the present-perfect tense, but know there are plenty of examples where they're different.

> *Ej.* está despierto, ha despertado (despertar)   está lleno, han llenado (llenar)
> está contento, han contentado (contentar)   está limpio, hemos limpiado (limpiar)

There is no apparent rhyme or reason to irregulars, so asking why verbs are irregular is pointless. In order to properly use *regular* past participles or any *regular* verb in a given verb tense, we must simply learn a set of rules and apply them to every regular verb. Irregulars are a little more difficult. The first thing we must understand is that irregulars are not optionally irregular; we must accept that they just are. Although we are able to categorize most of them, we must understand the nature of each category and all of its changes. Sometimes, we must learn the irregulars individually because they are unique and do not fit into any category. Take a look at some examples in Spanish.

- **Regulares:**

    Ej. Yo <u>he vivido</u> en Colorado por 6 años.   I have lived in Colorado for 6 years.
    ¿<u>Ha caminado</u> alguna vez a la escuela?   Has she ever walked to school?
    El tráfico <u>ha contribuido</u> al ruido.   Traffic has contributed to the noise.
    <u>Hemos intentado</u> sacar buenas notas.   We have tried to get good grades.
    ¿Cómo <u>has estado</u>?   How have you been?
    Ella <u>ha sido</u> muy responsable este año.   She has been very responsible this year.

- **Irregulares:**

    Ej. <u>He hecho</u> mi tarea.   I have done my homework.
    <u>Hemos escrito</u> muchos ensayos.   We have written a lot of essays.
    No <u>ha dicho</u> la verdad en su vida.   She hasn't told the truth in her life.
    Mis papás <u>han resuelto</u> su bronca.   My parents have resolved their problem.

- **Reflexivos:**

    Ej. <u>Se han inscrito</u> en sus clases.   They have signed up for their classes.
    <u>Me he roto</u> la pierna.   I have broken my leg.
    Mi abuelo ya <u>se ha muerto</u>.   My grandpa has already died.
    <u>Nos hemos puesto</u> los zapatos.   We have put on our shoes.
    <u>Se ha abrochado</u> su propio cinturón.   He has buckled his own seatbelt

Notice the placement of the reflexive pronouns (*me, te, se, nos, os, se*) in the above examples. You know from previous verb tenses (not commands) that object pronouns, whether reflexive, direct, or indirect, are placed immediately before a conjugated verb. In the case of the present-perfect tense, that conjugated verb is the verb *haber*. Take a look at some more complicated examples and notice the placement of the object pronouns. Notice that in the last two examples, the infinitive is used because the verb follows a preposition, and therefore the pronouns are attached to the end.

    Ej. Me los he puesto.   I have put them on.
    Te lo ha dicho mil veces.   He has told you a thousand times.
    …después de haberlo hecho.   …after having done it.
    …por habérmelas explicado.   …for having explained them to me.

¡Ojo! In all perfect tenses (*haber* + past participle), the past participle is an adverb and, therefore, does not have gender or number. This means that it always ends in *o*.

Unidad 22

Los verbos (el pluscuamperfecto) – Verbs (pluperfect tense)

The present-perfect tense (pp.64-65) is used to describe past actions or events that are still relevant to the present. The pluperfect tense is used to describe past actions or events that are prior to—and relevant to—another action or event in the past.

> *Ej.* I didn't go to the restaurant with them because I <u>had</u> (already) <u>eaten</u>.
> They <u>had washed</u> their hands before eating.

Take a look at some more examples of the pluperfect in English.

> *Ej.* I didn't buy the DVD when it came out because I <u>had</u> (already) <u>seen</u> the movie twice.
> She <u>had turned</u> in her report before her colleagues even started theirs.

The pluperfect, like the present perfect, is a compound tense because it has two components: a helping verb (to have) and the past participle of the verb you are conjugating. Whereas the present perfect uses the verb *haber* in the present tense, the pluperfect uses the verb *haber* in the imperfect tense. Remember, the past participle here is an adverb (no gender or number).

haber – to have (not possession)		**-ed**
había	habíamos	-ar → -ado
habías	habíais	-er → -ido
había	habían	-ir → -ido

Compare the examples above with their Spanish translations below:

> *Ej.* No fui al restaurante con ellos porque yo (ya) <u>había comido</u>.
> Ellos <u>se habían lavado</u> las manos antes de comer.
>
> Yo no compré el DVD cuando salió porque yo (ya) <u>había visto</u> la película dos veces.
> Ella <u>había entregado</u> su reportaje antes de que sus colegas aun empezaran los suyos.

See pages 62-65 for rules and examples concerning regular and irregular past participles as well as pronoun placement for perfect tenses. Below is a quick-reference summary. Notice the patterns of irregular past participles with the same verb roots.

- **Regulares: -ado** (jugado), **-ido** (bebido, vivido)

- **Irregulares: -to** (abierto, cubierto, escrito, inscrito, descrito, puesto, compuesto, impuesto, supuesto, visto, previsto, resuelto, vuelto, devuelto, envuelto, muerto, frito, roto), **-cho** (dicho, hecho, deshecho, satisfecho), **-so** (impreso, also imprimido)

¡Ojo! In perfect tenses, in Spanish, nothing can come between *haber* and the past participle, unlike in English: "I <u>had</u> already <u>seen</u> …" – *Yo había ~~ya~~ visto* … → *Yo ya había visto* …

Unidad 23

Los verbos (el futuro) – Verbs (future tense)

You've already learned how to talk about the future (pp.16, 54). *Ir* (in the present tense) + *a* + infinitive is a common way to talk about the future.

> *Ej.* <u>Voy a jugar</u> al golf mañana. – <u>I am going to play</u> golf tomorrow.
> ¿A qué hora <u>vas a cenar</u>? – What time <u>are you going to eat</u> dinner?

This is the compound form (multiple verbs). There is also a simple form (one verb) that is equally common. Unlike the other verb tenses you've studied so far, the endings in the future tense are the same whether the verb is *-ar*, *-er* or *-ir*. Also unlike the other verb tenses you've studied so far, regular verbs in the future tense are conjugated by adding the ending to the infinitive. Take a look at the following regular verbs in the future tense.

comprar – to buy		volver – to return	
compraré	compraremos	volveré	volveremos
comprarás	compraréis	volverás	volveréis
comprará	comprarán	volverá	volverán

> *Ej.* Mi tía <u>comprará</u> pronto un carro nuevo. – My aunt <u>will buy</u> a new car soon.
> No <u>volveremos</u> hasta medianoche. – We <u>won't return</u> until the middle of the night.

You can see in the examples above that the future tense is used to say what someone will or won't do. As with all verb tenses, there are irregular verbs and many of the irregulars in the future are the usual suspects from most other verb tenses. Although their endings are the same as the regulars, irregulars do not use the infinitive as a base. Below are the most common irregulars.

hacer (har) – to do / to make		poner (pondr) – to put / to set	
haré	haremos	pondré	pondremos
harás	haréis	pondrás	pondréis
hará	harán	pondrá	pondrán

poder (podr) – to be able		venir (vendr) – to come	
podré	podremos	vendré	vendremos
podrás	podréis	vendrás	vendréis
podrá	podrán	vendrá	vendrán

querer (querr) – to want		tener (tendr) – to have	
querré	querremos	tendré	tendremos
querrás	querréis	tendrás	tendréis
querrá	querrán	tendrá	tendrán

saber (sabr) – to know (info.)		decir (dir) – to say / to tell	
sabré	sabremos	diré	diremos
sabrás	sabréis	dirás	diréis
sabrá	sabrán	dirá	dirán

valer (valdr) – to be worth		salir (saldr) – to go out	
valdré	valdremos	saldré	saldremos
valdrás	valdréis	saldrás	saldréis
valdrá	valdrán	saldrá	saldrán

Los verbos (el futuro perfecto) – Verbs (future-perfect tense)

Now that you've seen two perfect tenses (present perfect and pluperfect), it should be easy to add the future perfect to your repertoire. This tense is used to talk about future events or actions that will have happened prior to—and relevant to—another future event or action. Try not to get bogged down by the timeline of these perfect tenses; your brain already knows what to do with them.

Ej. After my shift on Saturday night, I will have worked 60 hours this week.

If you take too long, you will have missed your chance.

As with all other perfect tenses, all you need for the future perfect is our ever-so-helpful "helping" verb, *haber*, conjugated in the future tense, and our now-familiar past participle. Notice that its conjugations are irregular like *saber*.

haber – to have (not possession)		-ed
habré	habremos	-ar → -ado
habrás	habréis	-er → -ido
habrá	habrán	-ir → -ido

Compare the examples above with their Spanish translations below:

Ej. Después de mi turno el sábado por la noche, habré trabajado 60 horas esta semana.

Si tardas demasiado, habrás perdido tu oportunidad.

Use this space to take a deep breath before the plunge ahead.

Or use it to draw a picture of your head exploding from imminent information overload.

Los verbos (el subjuntivo) – Verbs (subjunctive mood)

Do you remember commands (pp.55-58)? Of course you do! You may also remember them as the imperative mood. There are many verb tenses in Spanish, but there are also moods – three to be exact: the indicative, the imperative, and the subjunctive.

The **indicative mood** encompasses the majority of your understanding of verbs so far. It "indicates" when an action or event takes place: past, present, future, past of the past, past of the future, future of the past, etc. There are **nine verb tenses** in the indicative mood.

The **imperative mood**, or commands, is used to tell someone what to do. You may remember that since the one being ordered to carry out the action can refuse, forget, etc., the *when* of the action cannot be confirmed at the time of the command. This means that the imperative mood does not have verb tenses.

That leaves us with the **subjunctive mood**, which has cross-over with the above two moods. It is used to express doubt and uncertainty about whether or not an event or action will happen, fear and other emotions about an event or situation, hypothetical situations, as well as to indicate what one subject wants another subject to do. There are **four verb tenses** in the subjunctive mood, giving us **thirteen total verb tenses** to navigate in order to be fluent in Spanish.

The indicative and imperative moods are commonly used in English, but the subjunctive mood is all but dead, leaving us with very little to relate to when learning it in Spanish. While you can get by without using it yourself, I can assure you it is alive and well in Spanish and the better you understand it, the better you'll be able to communicate with native speakers. There is a huge learning curve with the subjunctive for native speakers of English, so be patient with yourself and get ready to shed a few tears.

The subjunctive mood is predominately used after the word *que*, indicating the introduction of a subordinate clause, so let's start there. In most cases, this *que* does not translate well into English, and in the cases in which it does translate, it is often omitted in English but cannot be omitted in Spanish. Enough lead-up; let's get to it.

How would you translate the following phrase: *Te quiero leer*?

Did you say, "I want you to read" (*Te quiero* – I want you, *leer* – to read)?

What about: *Quiero leerte*?

Did you say, "I want to read to you" (*Quiero* – I want, *leerte* – to read to you)?

Given what you've learned about the placement of object pronouns relative to verbs, whether conjugated or not (pp.11, 19, 22, 24-27, 36-43, 51-53), you have the prior knowledge to recognize that *te quiero leer* and *quiero leerte* are both grammatically correct ways to say the same thing. So, now you have to ask yourself which is the correct translation. Well, what else do you know that you can reference? What does *quiero leer* mean? "I want to read," right? So, no matter where we place the *te*, our phrase means, "I want to read to you."

The subjunctive mood is how "I want you to read" can be translated into Spanish. I cannot emphasize this enough: translating the subjunctive literally will not help you understand it. This is a great point in your studies to start thinking in Spanish, letting go of any dependence on thinking in English you may still have.

The imperative mood is used to tell someone what to do (*Lee.* – "Read."), but that can come off as a little harsh. An alternative is to express to someone what you want them to do without telling them directly to do it. Let's break down our sentence: "I want you to read."

"I want" is the indicative mood, present tense. That's easy – *Quiero.*

Next, *que* (literally "that," but I'm telling you it's going to sound stupid)

Then, finally, the subjunctive mood of the present tense (in this case) of the verb "to read," conjugated for the person we want to do it: *tú.* Similar to the imperative mood (commands), the person who wants the action to take place has no control over the outcome (grammatically speaking, that is), so the verb endings are the opposite of the indicative pattern, just like the imperative pattern (p.55).

Indicative pattern in the **present** tense: **-ar** (habl<u>ar</u>) → **-a** (habl<u>a</u>)

-er (le<u>er</u>) → -e (le<u>e</u>)

-ir (viv<u>ir</u>) → -e (viv<u>e</u>)

Subjunctive pattern in the **present** tense: **-ar** → **-e** (habl<u>e</u>)

-er → -a (le<u>a</u>)

-ir → -a (viv<u>a</u>)

Drum roll, please … (*Yo*) *quiero que* (*tú*) *le<u>as</u>.* (Don't make me translate it literally!)

Regardless of its translation, learn to think *que* when using the subjunctive and you'll be less likely to use it in the wrong context. Below are **regular** verbs, in the **present** of the **subjunctive** mood.

habl<u>ar</u>		**com<u>er</u>**		**viv<u>ir</u>**
que **habl<u>e</u>**	que	com<u>a</u>	que	viv<u>a</u>
que **habl<u>es</u>**	que	com<u>as</u>	que	viv<u>as</u>
que **habl<u>e</u>**	que	com<u>a</u>	que	viv<u>a</u>
que **habl<u>emos</u>**	que	com<u>amos</u>	que	viv<u>amos</u>
que **habl<u>éis</u>**	que	com<u>áis</u>	que	viv<u>áis</u>
que **habl<u>en</u>**	que	com<u>an</u>	que	viv<u>an</u>

¡Ojo! The *yo* and *él/ella/Ud.* forms are always the same as each other in the subjunctive mood.

> *Ej.* **Dese<u>an</u>** (indicative, not in dispute) *que* **limpi<u>emos</u>** los platos (subjunctive, in doubt).
> **Necesit<u>a</u>** (indicative, fact) *que* **escrib<u>as</u>** la carta (subjunctive, you may not comply).
> **Prefer<u>imos</u>** (indicative) *que* **habl<u>en</u>** con el jefe (subjunctive, they may or may not).
> **Esper<u>o</u>** (I hope) *que* **comprend<u>as</u>** un poco del subjuntivo (I won't hold my breath).
> **Pid<u>o</u>** (I ask) *que* **estudi<u>es</u>** un poco cada día (pretty please).

Unidad 24

Los verbos (el subjuntivo) – Verbs (subjunctive mood)

It's normal to over apply a rule or concept shortly after learning it. One example is being tempted to make every verb reflexive soon after learning the concept of reflexive pronouns. Another example is forgetting about the indicative mood and using the subjunctive mood for simple sentences. Be careful to not throw out what you already knew about showing desire.

When talking about what a subject wants to have happen, follow these two general rules:

➢ If one subject desires that another subject do something, use the subjunctive to show that the first subject has no grammatical control over the outcome.

> *Ej.* Los padres (subject #1) quieren **que** →
> sus hijos (subject #2) **coman** muchos vegetales.

¡Ojo! The above sentence does not indicate whether the parents' children eat a lot of vegetables or not. It doesn't indicate what their children do at all; it merely indicates what the parents want.

➢ If one subject desires to do the action, use the infinitive.

> *Ej.* Los padres (subject #1) quieren →
> **comer** (still same subject) muchos vegetales.

Showing what one subject wants another subject to do is only one use of the subjunctive. Expressing the speaker's doubt about whether something is real or whether something will happen is another use. Take a look at the two following statements. See if you can figure out why one uses the indicative and the other uses the subjunctive.

> *Ej.* Creo **que** →
> **va** (indicative) a llover hoy. – I believe (that) it is going to rain today.

> No creo **que** →
> **vaya** (subjunctive) a llover hoy. – I don't believe (that) it is going to rain today.

Would you agree that if we removed "I believe (that)" from the first example, the sentence, for all intents and purposes, would have the same meaning?

Would you agree that if we removed "I don't believe (that)" from the second example, the sentence would have the exact opposite meaning?

The speaker uses the subjunctive to negate or deny "it is going to rain." In English, we do not make this type of distinction, but in Spanish, it sounds pretty weird to deny something by saying, *no creo que*, and then immediately affirm what was just denied by stating, *va a llover*.

¡Ojo! Whether or not it rains does not matter grammatically. What matters is what the speaker believes or doesn't believe. The subjunctive here is all about the speaker's perspective.

When you're talking about what you believe, think, doubt, etc., put your statement to this test by deleting the main clause. If the meaning remains the same, you need the indicative. If it means the opposite of what you intended, you need the subjunctive.

Ej. Pienso que eres inteligente. → ~~Pienso que~~ eres inteligente. (same)

No creo que el bus viene a tiempo. → ~~No creo que~~ el bus viene a tiempo. (opposite)

The first example checks out, so *eres* (indicative) works. The second one, however, does not check out, so *viene* does **not** work. This is what the second example should look like:

No creo **que** el bus **venga** a tiempo.

Dudar means to doubt, so it will work like *no creer* or *no pensar*, whereas *no dudar* works like *creer* and *pensar*.

Ej. <u>Dudo</u> **que** el bus **venga** a tiempo. – I doubt the bus will arrive on time.
　　　　　　　　　　　　　　　　　　~~I doubt~~ the bus will arrive on time. (opposite)

<u>No dudo</u> **que eres** inteligente. – I don't doubt you are intelligent.
　　　　　　　　　　　　　　　　~~I don't doubt~~ you are intelligent. (same)

The subjunctive mood shares characteristics with both the indicative mood and the imperative mood. Here are a few things to keep in mind when conjugating the subjunctive.

➤ The placement of object pronouns is the same as the indicative: before the conjugated verb, attached to an infinitive, etc. (pp.11, 19, 22, 24-27, 36-43, 51-53).

Ej. No creo que **te vayas a acostar** temprano durante tus vacaciones.
No creo que **vayas a acostarte** temprano durante tus vacaciones.

➤ **Irregulars** in the subjunctive, like irregulars in the imperative, are based on the *yo* form in the present tense of the indicative (pp.56-58).

salir → <u>salg</u>o	Mi papá quiere **que yo salga** de la casa.
tener → <u>teng</u>o	Yo deseo **que tú tengas** tiempo para estudiar.
poner → <u>pong</u>o	No creo **que te pongas** una corbata para ir al gimnasio.
traer → <u>traig</u>o	Espero **que Estrella traiga** suficiente comida a la fiesta.
hacer → <u>hag</u>o	Dudo **que Jorge y Tomás hagan** mucho ejercicio.
ver → <u>ve</u>o	El maestro quiere **que tú y yo veamos** películas en español.
ir → voy	No quieres **que yo vaya** a México sin ti, ¿verdad?
venir → <u>veng</u>o	Esperamos **que tú vengas** a la fiesta este viernes.
decir → <u>dig</u>o	Necesito **que Uds. me digan** la verdad.
ser → soy	La mamá de Penélope quiere **que sea** médica.
saber → <u>sé</u>	Quiero **que tú sepas** que no estoy enojado contigo.

¡Ojo! The *yo* and *él/ella/Ud.* forms, are always the same as each other in the subjunctive mood, so it's much more important that you use subject pronouns to maintain clarity.

Los verbos irregulares (el subjuntivo del presente)

The following are complete charts of some of the irregular verbs on the previous page so that you can better see their patterns.

salir	tener	ver	ir	decir	ser
que salga	que tenga	que vea	que vaya	que diga	que sea
que salgas	que tengas	que veas	que vayas	que digas	que seas
que salga	que tenga	que vea	que vaya	que diga	que sea
que salgamos	que tengamos	que veamos	que vayamos	que digamos	que seamos
que salgáis	que tengáis	que veáis	que vayáis	que digáis	que seáis
que salgan	que tengan	que vean	que vayan	que digan	que sean

In addition to the irregulars mentioned above and on the previous page, there are stem-changing verbs in the present tense of the subjunctive, which are irregular like stem-changing verbs in the indicative, but with a twist for *-ir* verbs.

mostrar (o → ue) – to show

indicativo: muestro mostramos **subjuntivo:** que muestre que mostremos
muestras mostráis que muestres que mostréis
muestra muestran que muestre que muestren

volver (o → ue) – to return / to go back

indicativo: vuelvo volvemos **subjuntivo:** que vuelva que volvamos
vuelves volvéis que vuelvas que volváis
vuelve vuelven que vuelva que vuelvan

Just like in the indicative, the subjunctive forms of *-ar* and *-er* verbs are stem-changing in all forms except the *nosotros* and *vosotros* forms; *-ir* verbs, on the other hand, have a twist. In addition to the normal stem changes, the *nosotros* and *vosotros* forms *do* have a stem change, but it isn't the same as the present-tense change; it is the same stem change used in the preterite tense for *-ir* verbs (p.35) and the gerund (*-iendo* form) (p.47).

dormir (o → ue) (o → u) – to sleep

indicativo: duermo dormimos **subjuntivo:** que duerma que durmamos
duermes dormís que duermas que durmáis
duerme duermen que duerma que duerman

conseguir (e → i) (e → i) – to get – to acquire

indicativo: consigo conseguimos **subjuntivo:** que consiga que consigamos
consigues conseguís que consigas que consigáis
consigue consiguen que consiga que consigan

convertir (e → ie) (e → i) – to convert

indicativo: convierto convertimos **subjuntivo:** que convierta que convirtamos
conviertes convertís que conviertas que convirtáis
convierte convierten que convierta que conviertan

Los verbos (el subjuntivo o el indicativo) – Verbs (subjunctive or indicative mood)

In addition to the standard *que*, there are a few other words that introduce the subjunctive. Words like *posiblemente* (possibly), *probablemente* (probably), *quizá(s)* (maybe) and *tal vez* (perhaps), by definition, express a certain level of doubt. In these cases, when used before the verb, either the indicative or the subjunctive can be used. Some cultures use the subjunctive and indicative interchangeably with these words, whereas other cultures make a slight distinction based on the level of doubt. The phrase *no saber si* (to not know if/whether) can go either way, as well.

> *Ej.* Posiblemente viene este sábado. (said somewhat optimistically)
> Posiblemente venga este sábado. (said somewhat pessimistically)
>
> Probablemente tenemos tiempo después de clases. (90% chance)
> Probablemente tengamos tiempo después de clases. (70% chance)
>
> Quizá voy al cine con Uds. (Save me a spot.)
> Quizá vaya al cine con Uds. (Don't hold your breath.)
>
> Tal vez tomamos un cafecito el lunes que viene. (I'd like to.)
> Tal vez tomemos un cafecito el lunes que viene. (I'm not sure if you'd like to.)
>
> No sé si mi amiga viene/venga hoy. (The difference is more cultural than semantic).

¡Ojo! If the verb is used first, the indicative is obligatory.

> *Ej.* Viene posiblemente este sábado.
> ~~Venga posiblemente este sábado.~~ (Would be interpreted as an Ud. command.)

Another fun word is *aunque*. There is definitely more doubt when used with the subjunctive.

> *Ej.* No querré ir al cine el próximo viernes, aunque (*even if*) tenga bastante dinero.
> No quiero ir al cine el próximo viernes, aunque (*even though*) tengo bastante dinero.

Los verbos (el subjuntivo del presente perfecto)

The present-perfect tense in the subjunctive mood, as it is in the indicative mood, is used to talk about past actions or events that are relevant to the present moment. The difference, then, is the same difference we see in the present tense between the two moods: subordinate clause, preceded by *que*, expressing desire, preference, doubt, etc.

haber – to have (not possession)		-ed
que haya	que hayamos	-ar → -ado
que hayas	que hayáis	-er → -ido
que haya	que hayan	-ir → -ido

> *Ej.* No creo que <u>hayan ganado</u> la lotería.
> Prefieren que <u>hayamos comprado</u> los regalos antes de la fiesta.

Los verbos (el subjuntivo o el indicativo) – Verbs (subjunctive or indicative mood)

To say that learning the subjunctive mood is difficult would be an understatement. It is complicated, subtle, and, in some cases, subjective. Its subjectivity, in particular, makes it especially hard to master, even for native Spanish speakers. Most textbooks only give you 1st person examples of the subjunctive.

> *Ej.* <u>Creo</u> que los extraterrestres nos <u>han visitado</u>. (indicativo)
> <u>No creo</u> que los fantasmas <u>existan</u>. (subjuntivo)

The use of the subjunctive here is straightforward because the subject (*yo*) is the speaker. But what happens when the subject of the sentence is different from the speaker? Whose belief or doubt is expressed: the subject's or speaker's?

> *Ej.* Mi hermana cree que los extraterrestres nos <u>han visitado</u>. (indicativo)
> Mi hermana cree que los extraterrestres nos <u>hayan visitado</u>. (subjuntivo)

Both of the above examples are grammatically correct, although the second one may sound strange even to some native speakers. In the first one, the speaker probably has no contrary belief worth mentioning. In the second, the speaker believes his/her sister is crazy.

> *Ej.* Mi amigo no cree que los fantasmas <u>existan</u>. (subjuntivo)
> Mi amigo no cree que los fantasmas <u>existen</u>. (indicativo)

The examples above are grammatically correct. In the first one, the speaker probably has the same belief as the friend. In the second, the speaker cannot believe his/her friend is so skeptical.

> *Ej.* ¿Crees que los extraterrestres <u>existen</u>? (The speaker hasn't made up his/her mind.)
> ¿Crees que los extraterrestres <u>existan</u>? (The speaker obviously doesn't believe it.)
> No creas/pienses que <u>soy</u> tonta. (To tell someone what not to think, use the indicative.)

Another way the subjunctive is used is to show interest in something or someone that the speaker acknowledges may or may not exist, and may even fantasize about.

> *Ej.* ¿Tienes un lápiz que me <u>prestes</u>? (prestar – to lend)
> Quiero un trabajo que me <u>pague</u> mucho dinero y me <u>dé</u> seis semanas de vacaciones.
> Necesito unos amigos a quienes les <u>encante</u> viajar.
> Busco una novia que <u>sea</u> muy bonita y <u>tenga</u> un buen sentido de humor.
> ¿Hay alguien que <u>lea</u> poesía? (No hay nadie que <u>lea</u> poesía.)

In these examples above, the speaker doesn't have any particular pencil, job, friends, girlfriend, or "someone" in mind. For "no hay nadie" (or "no hay nada"), the subjunctive is used to show that the speaker acknowledges that there is no way to verify such a bold statement.

¡Ojo! The "personal *a*" (p.52) does not apply to the above examples since they are impersonal, however, two exceptions are the words *nadie* (no one/anyone) and *alguien* (someone).

> *Ej.* No conozco **a** nadie que <u>sepa</u> (saber) japonés.
> Busco **a** alguien que <u>hable</u> alemán.

Unidad 25

Los verbos (el subjuntivo o el indicativo) – Verbs (subjunctive or indicative mood)

You've now seen two very different uses of the subjunctive. The first one was to show desire (pp.69-71) and the second one was to show doubt or lack of belief (pp.71-72). Instead of trying to memorize every type of example, let's proceed by breaking the subjunctive down into two categories: **head** and **heart**.

- **Head**

Understanding – creer, pensar, comprender, entender, reconocer, opinar, considerar, suponer, imaginar(se), figurarse, comprobar, saber, deducir, recordar, acordarse (de), averiguar, descubrir, adivinar, soñar, intuir, estar seguro (de), estar convencido (de), etc. + *que*

Senses – ver, oír, notar, observar, comprobar, darse cuenta (de), descubrir, sentir, etc. + *que*

Language – decir, admitir, contar, afirmar, narrar, escribir, comunicar, referir, confesar, murmurar, susurrar, explicar, manifestar, contestar, revelar, jurar, prometer, sostener, indicar, responder, comentar, declarar, relatar, señalar, leer, mencionar, etc. + *que*

Basic Rules:

➤ If verb 1 is affirmative, then <u>verb 2</u> requires the indicative.
    Ej. Creo que <u>es</u> buena idea.
       Veo que <u>tienes</u> un carro nuevo.

➤ If verb 1 is negative, then <u>verb 2</u> requires the subjunctive.
    Ej. No creo que <u>sea</u> buena idea.
       No admito que <u>tengas</u> mejor carro que yo.

Impersonal Statements – ser, ser evidente, ser cierto, ser indudable, ser indiscutible, ser obvio, ser verdad, ser seguro, estar claro, estar visto, estar demostrado, dar la impresión (de), verse, notarse, resultar, pasar, suceder, etc. + *que*

    Ej. Es evidente que tú <u>has</u> aprendido mucho.
       Es verdad que <u>es</u> difícil aprender el subjuntivo.

       No está claro que <u>hayas</u> aprendido el subjuntivo.
       No es obvio que <u>sea</u> fácil aprender el subjuntivo.

       ¿Es que no te <u>gusta</u> el ajo?
       No, no es que el ajo no me <u>guste</u>, sino que siempre <u>ponen</u> demasiado.

- **Heart**

Emotions – gustar, encantar, avergonzarse, molestar, fastidiar, dar pena, contentarse con, conformarse con, cansarse de, hartarse de, resignarse a, sufrir, aguantar, soportar, extrañar, admirar, consolar, doler, aburrir, divertir, entusiasmar, alegrar, alegrarse (de), entristecer, apenar, lamentar, quejarse de, temer, tener miedo de, sentir, estar temeroso de, estar asombrado de, estar sorprendido (de), estar satisfecho (de), tener interés en … + *que*

Will or Desire – esperar, querer, desear, preferir, aspirar a, pretender, intentar, apetecer, oponerse a, conseguir, lograr, hacer (lograr) … + *que*

Commands, Advice, Pleas, Prohibition – decir (ordenar), ordenar, mandar, decretar, aconsejar, desaconsejar, recomendar, animar a, invitar a, incitar a, pedir, rogar, suplicar, solicitar, procurar, permitir, consentir, dejar, acceder a, prohibir, impedir, obligar a, hacer (obligar), exigir … + *que*

Other Verbs – interesar, ayudar a, esperar a, tolerar, contribuir a, aventurarse a, exponerse a, criticar, aprobar, estar decidido a, estar acostumbrado a, estar dispuesto a … + *que*

Basic Rules:

➢ Whether verb 1 is affirmative or negative, <u>verb 2</u> requires the subjunctive.
   Ej. Quiero que <u>salgas</u>.
      No quiero que <u>salgas</u>.

➢ If verb 1 and verb 2 refer to the same person, then <u>verb 2</u> requires the infinitive.
   Ej. Quiero <u>salir</u>.
      No quieren <u>salir</u>.

Impersonal Statements – (no) ser bueno, ser malo, ser mejor, ser peor, ser fácil, ser difícil, ser raro, ser necesario, ser curioso, ser extraño, estar bien, estar mal, ser (in)útil, ser (im)probable, poder, ser (im)posible, ser estupendo, ser maravilloso, ser esencial, ser sorprendente, ser natural, ser (in)justo, ser estúpido, ser ridículo, ser terrible, ser horroroso, ser (i)lógico, ser una pena, ser imprescindible, ser indispensable, ser una (des)ventaja, ser una locura, ser una barbaridad, ser una coincidencia, ser una tontería, ser una lástima, parecer mentira, ser hora de, ser tiempo de, no haber (la menor) posibilidad (esperanza, oportunidad, etc.) de, bastar, hacer falta, convenir, tener derecho a, poder ser, dar pena (rabia, gusto, alegría, tristeza, vergüenza …), valer más … + *que*

   Ej. Es bueno que estudies español.
      No es bueno que te frustres.

   Ej. Es bueno estudiar español. (universal statement)
      No es bueno frustrarse. (universal statement)

Additional Expressions: para, con el fin de, a menos, a no ser, con tal de, acaso, sin … + *que*

¡Ojo! In certain cases, verb 1 can be omitted, often when no one has control of the outcome.
   Ej. Que te mejores pronto. Que les vaya bien. Que tengan un bonito día.

Los verbos (el subjuntivo o el indicativo) – Verbs (subjunctive or indicative mood)

You might have noticed that a few verbs appear on both lists (head/heart). This is not a mistake. The distinction between the two hangs solely on the use of the subjunctive or indicative.

Sentir – You can feel with your heart as well as with your physical senses.

> *Ej.* Siento que tengas frío. (corazón – empatía) – I'm sorry you are cold.
> Siento que tienes frío. (cabeza – percepción) – I sense/perceive/see that you are cold.

Decir – You can relate what someone tells you to do, which shows desire in the form of an indirect command, but you can also relate what someone's physical senses perceive.

> *Ej.* "Me dice que corra rápidamente." (corazón – indirect command/desire) – subjunctive
> ("Me dice, 'Corre rápidamente.'") – imperativo (mandato)
>
> "Me dice que corro rápidamente." (cabeza – información/belief) – indicative
> ("Me dice, 'Corres rápidamente.'") – indicativo (presente)

- **Routine vs. Future**

Although most conjugations in the subjunctive mood follow the word *que*, it isn't always the case. The words *cuando* (when), *en cuanto/tan pronto como* (as soon as) can either indicate a routine action/event or a future action/event. When used to talk about **routine** actions/events, the **indicative** is required. When used to talk about **future** action, the **subjunctive** is required, no matter how certain you are that the event will occur.

> *Ej.* <u>When</u> I travel abroad, I usually prefer Latin America. (routine)
> I always brush my teeth <u>as soon as</u> I get up in the morning. (routine)
>
> She's going to go out for a run <u>as soon as </u>the sun comes up tomorrow. (future)
> I'll buy a new car <u>when</u> I win the lottery next week. (future)

The first two are examples of routine, and you already know how to narrate your daily routine fairly well. The second two examples are both future. The sun will come up tomorrow and that is a fact of science. It is not a fact, however, that I will win the lottery next week. Grammatically, though, these are the same concept. It may not be a question of *if* but rather a question of exactly *when*. That uncertainty is the reason for the subjunctive. Let's see the translations.

> *Ej.* <u>Cuando</u> viajo (indicativo) al extranjero, normalmente prefiero Latinoamérica.
> Siempre me cepillo los dientes <u>en cuanto</u> me levanto (indicativo) en la mañana.
>
> Ella va a salir a correr <u>tan pronto como</u> salga (subjuntivo) el sol mañana.
> Compraré un carro nuevo <u>cuando</u> gane (subjuntivo) la lotería la próxima semana.

*¡Ojo! **Después de que*** requires the subjunctive when referring to the future and the indicative when referring to a routine or past sequence. ***Antes de que*** always requires the subjunctive.

Unidad 26

Los verbos (el subjuntivo) – Verbs (subjunctive mood)

Although mastering the subjunctive mood may (*definitely will*) take you years, hopefully you are starting to get a feel for its subtle and sometimes subjective nature.

You know the subjunctive usually follows the word *que*, and can follow the word *cuando* (p.78), but it can also follow the words *donde, como, quien(es)*, and *cuanto/a(s)*. Often these words are followed by the subjunctive form of the verb *ser* (*sea/sean*). This structure is used to express indifference to a choice and/or to defer to another person to make a decision.

> *Ej. lo que sea* – whatever (it may be)
> *cuando sea* – whenever (it may be)
> *cuanto/a sea / cuantos/as sean* – however much/many (it/they may be)
> *donde sea* – wherever (it may be)
> *como sea* – however (it may be)
> *quien sea / quienes sean* – whoever (it/they may be)

While it's one of the most common verbs to use in this context, *ser* isn't the only verb that can be used. The verb *querer* is also very common.

> *Ej. lo que (ella) quiera* – whatever she wants (what she wants remains to be seen)
> *cuando quieran* – whenever you (all) want
> *cuanto queramos* – however much we want
> *donde (yo) quiera* – wherever I want
> *como queráis* – however you (all) want
> *a quien quieras* – to whomever you want

In certain contexts, the words *cuando, cuanto, donde, como, cual(es)*, and *quien(es)* can be combined with the word *quiera* (the subjunctive of *querer*).

> *Ej. cuandoquiera* – whenever   *dondequiera* – wherever
> *cuantoquiera* – however much   *quienquiera / quienesquiera* – whoever
> *comoquiera* – however   *cualquiera / cualesquiera* – whichever

Cualquiera serves as a pronoun (by itself) or as an adjective (with a noun). When used before a noun, the final *a* is dropped: *cualquier cosa, cualesquier coches*. You have surely seen words whose endings are dropped before nouns: *grande → gran hombre, primero → primer piso*.

The following are similar expressions using the subjunctive:

> *Ej. Pase lo que pase, ...* – Whatever happens, …
> *Sea quien sea, ...* – Whoever it is, …
> *Hagas lo que hagas, ...* – Whatever you do, …
>
> *Por mucho que intentes, ...* – No matter how much you try, …
> *Por más lejos que vayamos, ...* – No matter how far (away) we go, …

Los verbos (el pretérito vs. el imperfecto)

Unlike in English, Spanish has two simple past tenses: the preterite (pp.28-29) and the imperfect (pp.48-49). As with *por/para*, *ser/estar/haber*, and *saber/conocer*, thinking in English will not help you understand their differences. Mastering their uses takes a lot of exposure and a keen ear. There are certain words and contexts that require one or the other, but sometimes it's a subjective choice. The more control you have over these tenses, the more precisely you'll be able to convey what you mean to convey and the greater the subtleties you'll be able to perceive.

- **Use the preterite:**
    - to tell what events/actions took place.
        Fui al club y me divertí bailando.
    - to inform that an event/action happened a definite number of times.
        Salió a correr seis veces la semana pasada.
    - to talk about the duration of an event/action (even if it wasn't an action).
        Estuvimos en el centro comercial por tres horas.
    - to tell of an event or action that had a definitive start and stop.
        Viste la tele de las 19:00 a las 23:30 anoche.
    - to talk about a series of events that can be grouped together as one.
        Nuestro equipo de fútbol jugó muy mal el año pasado (varios partidos).
    - to convey a causal relationship between events/actions.
        Ella salió corriendo cuando vio al ladrón.

- **Use the imperfect:**
    - to paint an image of the background or scene surrounding the events or actions.
        Era una noche lluviosa y oscura. El viento silbaba y el cielo tronaba.
    - to describe habitual actions or actions that happened an indefinite number of times.
        De niña, ella jugaba en el parque todos los fines de semana.
    - to describe action that was in progress when an event occurred.
        Yo nadaba (estaba nadando) en la piscina cuando oí la alarma.
    - to reference what a printed text said (the text doesn't cease to inform once you read it).
        El artículo decía que los supervivientes fueron trasladados al refugio.
    - to blur the clarity of an event/action that would conventionally require the use of the preterite. This is a technique used in journalism to remove the focus from an event/action to create contrast with and focus on events deemed more important to the story. For their vague and blurry nature, dreams are often narrated in the imperfect.

The preterite takes the reader forward in time from one event to another. The imperfect pauses the action and allows the reader to stop, look around, and imagine. When narrating a story, there is always a balance to be struck between the preterite and the imperfect. If you give too much background information with the imperfect, your reader may lose interest before the events/actions of the story take place. If you don't give enough background information and go straight to the exciting events of the story, your reader will fail to picture the scene and, consequently, have a hard time empathizing with the characters and/or struggle to understand their motivations.

¡Ojo! Although common in English, the conditional tense in Spanish (p.81) cannot be used to talk about past routine. Instead, the imperfect is used.

> *Ej.* As a kid, I would often play all day. – De niño, yo a menudo ~~jugaría~~ jugaba todo el día.

Unidad 27

Los verbos (el condicional) – Verbs (conditional tense)

You've already seen the future tense (p.67), which is obviously used to talk about the future of the present, but what about the future of the past? Although you might not have considered this concept previously, you've certainly applied it perfectly thousands of times before. Consider this exchange between two co-workers on a random Monday morning:

> *Ej.* María: When do you think <u>you'll (you will) hand in</u> your report?
> Esteban: Don't worry; <u>I'll (I will) hand it in</u> by Wednesday morning.

Since Wednesday is still in the future as of this exchange, it makes sense to use the future tense. Now let's flash forward to Thursday and see what happens to the verb tense.

> *Ej.* María: You told me <u>you'd (you would) hand in</u> your report by yesterday morning.
> Esteban: I'm sorry; I really thought <u>I'd (I would) be able to</u> …

Now that the once future is the past, we have to adjust our verb tense to correspond. Not coincidentally, given their relation, the conditional tense follows the same rules and exceptions as the future tense; only its endings are different.

compr<u>ar</u> – to buy		volv<u>er</u> – to return	
comprar<u>ía</u>	comprar<u>íamos</u>	volver<u>ía</u>	volver<u>íamos</u>
comprar<u>ías</u>	comprar<u>íais</u>	volver<u>ías</u>	volver<u>íais</u>
comprar<u>ía</u>	comprar<u>ían</u>	volver<u>ía</u>	volver<u>ían</u>

Let's look again at that exchange, this time in Spanish.

> *Ej.* María: ¿Para cuándo piensas que <u>entregarás</u> tu reportaje? (futuro)
> Esteban: No te preocupes; lo <u>entregaré</u> para el miércoles por la mañana. (futuro)
>
> María: Me dijiste que <u>entregarías</u> tu reportaje para ayer. (condicional)
> Esteban: Disculpa; de verdad pensé que <u>podría</u> … (condicional)

All irregulars in the future tense have the same irregular roots in the conditional tense. Here's a review with conditional endings.

hacer (har) – to do / to make		**poner (pondr) – to put / to set**	
har<u>ía</u>	har<u>íamos</u>	pondr<u>ía</u>	pondr<u>íamos</u>
har<u>ías</u>	har<u>íais</u>	pondr<u>ías</u>	pondr<u>íais</u>
har<u>ía</u>	har<u>ían</u>	pondr<u>ía</u>	pondr<u>ían</u>

poder (podr) – to be able		
querer (querr) – to want	-ía	-íamos
tener (tendr) – to have	-ías	-íais
venir (vendr) – to come	-ía	-ían
saber (sabr) – to know (information)		
salir (saldr) – to go out		

Los verbos (el subjuntivo del imperfecto)

Remember, the subjunctive isn't a verb tense, but rather a mood. We have studied the subjunctive of the present tense, but there is also a subjunctive of the past (imperfect) tense, too. Its rules and uses are the same as in the present (head/heart), but its conjugations are obviously different.

	hablar		**comer**		**vivir**
que	hablara	que	comiera	que	viviera
que	hablaras	que	comieras	que	vivieras
que	hablara	que	comiera	que	viviera
que	habláramos	que	comiéramos	que	viviéramos
que	hablarais	que	comierais	que	vivierais
que	hablaran	que	comieran	que	vivieran

Remember, the *nosotros* form in the imperfect always has an accent mark whether the verb is regular, irregular, *-ar*, *-er*, or *-ir*.

Los verbos irregulares (el subjuntivo del imperfecto)

By now, you are no stranger to the concept of irregular verbs. Verb tenses (*voy, fui, iba, querrá*), commands (*pon, haz*), past participles (*visto, dicho*), and even the gerund (*durmiendo, pidiendo*) have irregular forms. The subjunctive of the imperfect is no exception. The good thing is that its irregular forms are not new; you've seen them in multiple contexts already: *durmió, durmiendo, que durmamos*. Let the *ellos/ellas/Uds.* form in the preterite be your guide.

ir/ser (fueron)	**querer (quisieron)**	**decir (dijeron)**	**dormir (durmieron)**
que fuera	que quisiera	que dijera	que durmiera
que fueras	que quisieras	que dijeras	que durmieras
que fuera	que quisiera	que dijera	que durmiera
que fuéramos	que quisiéramos	que dijéramos	que durmiéramos
que fuerais	que quisierais	que dijerais	que durmierais
que fueran	que quisieran	que dijeran	que durmieran

estar (estuvieron)	**saber (supieron)**	**dar (dieron)**	**pedir (pidieron)**
que estuviera	que supiera	que diera	que pidiera
que estuvieras	que supieras	que dieras	que pidieras
que estuviera	que supiera	que diera	que pidiera
que estuviéramos	que supiéramos	que diéramos	que pidiéramos
que estuvierais	que supierais	que dierais	que pidierais
que estuvieran	que supieran	que dieran	que pidieran

These are just a few of the many irregular verbs you've studied in the preterite. As I hope you can appreciate, this guide cannot possibly cover everything there is to know in the Spanish language. That said, I invite you to explore the *Real Academia Española* (www.rae.es) as it is, undoubtedly, the most highly regarded Spanish-language resource in existence. It gives you access to the most comprehensive dictionaries, which will hopefully be of great future use to you. In addition, it has a complete verb conjugator (search the verb in the dictionary and click the blue "*conjugar*" button).

Los verbos (el infinitivo o el subjuntivo)

As you already know (pp.69-70), *quiero leerte*, and *quiero que leas* are significantly different. They need to be so that you know who is expected to read. There are a few verbs, however, that, although the subjunctive may be used, the infinitive can also be used and the meaning remains the same. This is due to the nature of the verbs. While it is common to want to do something to someone else, it's not common to allow yourself, advise yourself, help yourself, teach yourself, prohibit yourself, etc, therefore there is no confusion as to who is to do the action.

> *Ej.* Déjame leer. / Deja(me) que (yo) lea. – Let me read. (dejar)
> Nos permitió salir. / (Nos) permitió que saliéramos. (permitir)
> Te aconsejo estudiar. / (Te) aconsejo que estudies. (aconsejar)
> Me hizo correr. / (Me) hizo que (yo) corriera. (hacer)

Other verbs commonly used both ways are: *recomendar*, *sugerir*, and *prohibir*.
Some verbs, like *ir*, require the preposition *a* regardless of which construction you use.

> *Ej.* Me obligó <u>a</u> buscarte. / (Me) obligó <u>a</u> que (yo) te buscara. (obligar)
> Nos pone <u>a</u> trabajar. / (Nos) pone <u>a</u> que trabajemos. (poner)
> Te voy <u>a</u> ayudar <u>a</u> estudiar. / (Te) voy <u>a</u> ayudar <u>a</u> que estudies. (ayudar)

Other verbs commonly used both ways that require an *a*, are: *invitar <u>a</u>*, *mandar <u>a</u>*, *incitar <u>a</u>*, and *enseñar <u>a</u>*. There is no limit to how many verbs you can string together. Don't forget your *a* if it's required.

> *Ej.* Pepa va <u>a</u> obligarme <u>a</u> permirtirte ayudar a Pedro <u>a</u> enseñarle a Paco <u>a</u> nadar.
> Pepa va <u>a</u> obligar <u>a</u> que yo permita que ayudes <u>a</u> que Pedro le enseñe <u>a</u> que Paco nade.

The syntax (word order) of the above phrases is correct either way you word it. Their meaning: "Pepa is going to make me allow you to help Pedro teach Paco to swim." Twice, in the first example above, you see an *a* that is not underlined. These are the "personal *a*."

Los verbos (el infinitivo o el indicativo)

With verbs of perception: *ver*, *mirar*, *oír*, *escuchar*, *sentir*, *observar*, etc., you can use either the infinitive or the indicative. The meaning is slightly different, but both work grammatically.

> *Ej.* Te vi entrar por la puerta trasera. – I saw you come in through the back door.
> Vi que entraste por la puerta trasera. – I saw (that) you came in through the back door.
> Te vi cuando entraste por … – I saw you when you came in through the back door.
>
> Me oyeron gritar. – They heard me shout.
> Oyeron que grité. – They heard (that) I shouted.
> Me oyeron cuando grité. – They heard me when I shouted.
>
> Te sentí tocarme el pelo. – I felt you touch my hair.
> Sentí que me tocaste el pelo. – I felt (that) you touched my hair.
> Te sentí cuando me tocaste el pelo. – I felt you when you touched my hair.

Unidad 28

Los verbos (las situaciones hipotéticas) – Verbs (hypothetical situations)

As you've seen (p.81), the conditional tense can be used as the future of the past, but that isn't its only use. It can also be used to hypothesize what *would* happen under certain "conditions."

Ej. What <u>would you do</u> with a million dollars?
Where <u>would you like</u> to go on vacation?
<u>I could eat</u> ten hotdogs in ten minutes.

These examples require the conditional tense because, in its most literal sense, certain conditions are required to carry out the action. Take a look at the translations of the above examples.

Ej. ¿Qué <u>harías</u> con un millón de dólares?
¿Adónde te <u>gustaría</u> ir de vacaciones?
(Yo) <u>podría</u> comer diez salchichas en diez minutos.

These statements above are simple, but many hypothetical statements include an "**if**" clause.

Ej. <u>If I had</u> a million dollars (I don't), I'd buy a new house.
I'd love to play golf <u>if my back didn't hurt</u> so much (but it does).

Even though these statements use the past tense in English, you instinctively know they are statements about the present. It is the same in Spanish, although the past tense is subjunctive of the imperfect.

Ej. <u>Si tuviera</u> un millón de dólares (no lo tengo), compraría una casa nueva.
Me encantaría jugar al golf <u>si la espalda no me doliera</u> tanto (pero sí me duele).

If the hypothetical is **present**, use the formula: *si* + **imperfect subjunctive** and **conditional**. But what if the hypothetical is past? That's where the final two perfect tenses come in handy.

condicional perfecto		subjuntivo del pluscuamperfecto	
habría	habríamos	que hubiera	que hubiéramos
habrías	habríais	que hubieras	que hubierais
habría	habrían	que hubiera	que hubieran

If the hypothetical is **past**, use: *si* + **pluperfect subjunctive** and **conditional perfect**.

Ej. <u>If I had won</u> the lottery drawing (I didn't), I would have bought a new house.
I would have played golf <u>if I hadn't hurt</u> my back (but I did).

These statements use perfect tenses to show their past nature. Check them out in Spanish.

Ej. <u>Si hubiera ganado</u> la lotería (no la gané), habría comprado una casa nueva.
Habría jugado al golf <u>si no me hubiera lastimado</u> la espalda (pero sí me la lastimé).

Los verbos (el subjuntivo del imperfecto)

Although they are much less common, it's worth mentioning that there are alternate endings for the subjunctive in the imperfect. You should focus on mastering the conjugations you've already seen (p.82), but don't be surprised if you hear one of the conjugations below from time to time.

	hablar		comer		vivir
que	hablase	que	comiese	que	viviese
que	hablases	que	comieses	que	vivieses
que	hablase	que	comiese	que	viviese
que	hablásemos	que	comiésemos	que	viviésemos
que	hablaseis	que	comieseis	que	vivieseis
que	hablasen	que	comiesen	que	viviesen

Of course, don't forget your irregulars.

ir/ser (fueron)	querer (quisieron)	decir (dijeron)	dormir (durmieron)
que fuese	que quisiese	que dijese	que durmiese
que fueses	que quisieses	que dijeses	que durmieses
que fuese	que quisiese	que dijese	que durmiese
que fuésemos	que quisiésemos	que dijésemos	que durmiésemos
que fueseis	que quisieseis	que dijeseis	que durmieseis
que fuesen	que quisiesen	que dijesen	que durmiesen

estar (estuvieron)	saber (supieron)	dar (dieron)	pedir (pidieron)
que estuviese	que supiese	que diese	que pidiese
que estuvieses	que supieses	que dieses	que pidieses
que estuviese	que supiese	que diese	que pidiese
que estuviésemos	que supiésemos	que diésemos	que pidiésemos
que estuvieseis	que supieseis	que dieseis	que pidieseis
que estuviesen	que supiesen	que diesen	que pidiesen

And the alternate pluperfect subjunctive forms must be:

que hubiese, hubieses, hubiese, hubiésemos, hubieseis, hubiesen + past participle

In English, the phrase "as if" followed by the subjunctive is commonly replaced with "like" followed by the indicative. Perhaps this is due to the demise of the subjunctive in English.

> *Ej.* He's goofing around *as if* I had all day to wait.
> He's goofing around *like* I have all day to wait.

Since the subjunctive is alive and well in Spanish, these phrases use *como si* followed by the subjunctive of the imperfect to show that the statement is not true.

> *Ej.* Está haciendo monerías *como si* yo tuviera/tuviese todo el día para esperar.
> Está haciendo monerías *como yo tengo* todo el día para esperar.

Los verbos (el subjuntivo – presente y pasado)

As previously stated, the rules and uses of the subjunctive are not tense specific; they apply the same for the present as they do for the past. As with the indicative, you can mix and match your verb tenses based on what you are trying to communicate. Mind your "head" and "heart" verbs.

> *Ej.* <u>Creo</u> que mi tío <u>fue</u> al banco ayer. (presente/pasado)
> <u>No creo</u> que mi tío <u>fuera</u> al banco ayer.
>
> <u>Parece</u> que mi tío <u>ha ido</u> al banco (porque no está aquí ahora).
> <u>No parece</u> que mi tío <u>haya ido</u> al banco (porque todavía está aquí).
>
> <u>Era obvio</u> cuando te conocí que <u>tenías</u> un buen sentido de humor. (pasado/pasado)
> <u>No me sorprendió</u> cuando te conocí que <u>fueras</u> comediante profesional.

Likewise, you can mix and match your tenses when talking about hypothetical situations.

> *Ej.* Si estudiara más (este semestre),
> estaría sacando una buena nota en clase (ahora).
> Si hubiera estudiado más (el semestre pasado),
> habría sacado una buena nota en clase (el semestre pasado).
> Si hubiera estudiado más (anoche),
> no estaría teniendo tantos problemas con este examen (ahora).

Los verbos (el subjuntivo o el indicativo) – Verbs (subjunctive or indicative mood)

As you might remember, when it comes to expressing belief and doubt, the use of the subjunctive is dependent on the speaker's doubt, not the subject's within the sentence. (p.75) What may look like a breaking of the "basic rules" of "head" verbs (p.76) is really a matter of perspective. In that same vein, when talking about the past, we can break from the rules when the speaker presently believes or knows something that he/she previously did not.

> *Ej.* Pepe: Hoy es mi cumpleaños.
> Marta: Ay, Pepe, siento no haberte comprado nada. <u>No sabía</u> *que* <u>era</u> tu cumple.

What Marta is saying with the use of the indicative is that although she didn't know before, she does now, thus there is no need for the subjunctive, even though the "head" verb is negative.

> *Ej.* Pepe: ¡Sabías que ayer cumplí 18 años!
> Marta: No, yo <u>no sabía</u> *que* <u>cumplieras</u> 18 años.

What Marta is saying with the use of the subjunctive is that she not only didn't know, but that she's not too sure about it even now. Whether it was or wasn't Pepe's birthday yesterday is not grammatically relevant. What *is* relevant is Marta's perspective now and, in this case, she rejects Pepe's claim that she knew yesterday was his birthday.

Los verbos (el indicativo y el subjuntivo)

As previously stated (p.69), there are nine verb tenses in the indicative mood and four (*) in the subjunctive mood. That means there is not a unique corresponding tense in the subjunctive mood for every unique tense in the indicative mood; they have to share. The following chart shows the corresponding tenses.

Indicativo:

    1. **presente** →
    2. **futuro** →

Ej. Creo que Miguel <u>es</u> alto. (presente) →
    No dudo que <u>hará</u> sol mañana. (futuro) →

    3. **presente perfecto** →
    4. **futuro perfecto** →

Ej. Es cierto que <u>han ganado</u>. (pres. perfecto) →
    Es indudable que <u>habrá comido</u>. (fut. perf.) →

    5. **pretérito** →
    6. **imperfecto** →
    7. **condicional** →

Ej. Es evidente que les <u>gustó</u>. (pretérito) →
    Es obvio que <u>estaba</u> feliz. (imperfecto) →
    Estaba claro que <u>querrían</u>. (condicional) →

    8. **pluscuamperfecto** →
    9. **condicional perfecto** →

Ej. Quizá lo <u>había visto</u>. (pluscuamperfecto) →
    Probablemente <u>habría ido</u>. (cond. perfecto) →

Subjuntivo:

1. **presente**

No creo que Miguel <u>sea</u> alto. (presente)
Dudo que <u>haga</u> sol mañana. (presente)

2. **presente perfecto**

No es cierto que <u>hayan ganado</u>. (pres. perf.)
Es dudable que <u>haya comido</u>. (pres. perf.)

3. **imperfecto**

Es absurdo que les <u>gustara</u>. (imperfecto)
Es curioso que <u>estuviera</u> feliz. (imperfecto)
No estaba claro que <u>quisieran</u>. (imperfecto)

4. **pluscuamperfecto**

Quizá lo <u>hubiera visto</u>. (pluscuamperfecto)
Posiblemente <u>hubiera ido</u>. (pluscuamperfecto)

* There is actually a fifth subjunctive form (future subjunctive), but it is virtually obsolete (like the subjunctive in English). It is used today only in legal documents and traditional sayings, but you might come across it some day in classic literature.

    Ej. Allá donde <u>fueres</u>, haz lo que <u>vieres</u>. ("When in Rome, do as the Romans do.")

Unidad 29

La descripción avanzada

Gender and number, adjective-noun agreement, and adjective placement are essential and fundamental pieces of the Spanish language. You already have the tools to understand their basic applications (pp.7, 18), but between the breaking of basic rules and the faithful application of advanced rules, there are plenty of subtleties to be learned in the name of linguistic mastery.

- **Nouns and their gender**

You already know that many nouns end in *e* or a consonant and that learning their definite articles (*el, la*) helps you learn the gender of these nouns. You also know that most nouns that end in *o* are masculine and most that end in *a* are feminine. I say "most," of course, because there are exceptions. Let's look at a few different types of rule breakers.

> *Ej.* el planeta, el mapa, la mano, el día, el sofá, el papá, el yoga, la libido, etc.

The above examples break the rules for different reasons. Some words ending in **ma** are masculine (due to their non-Latin origins), while others are feminine (of Latin origin).

> **Masculine**: el sistema, fantasma, problema, drama, idioma, tema, clima, poema, etc.
> **Feminine**: la forma, plataforma, pluma, paloma, goma, gama, fama, dama, mamá, etc.

In some cases, the masculine form means one thing and the feminine form means another.

> *Ej.* **el** cometa – comet, **el** coma – coma, **el** papa – pope, **el** capital – capital (money), etc.
> **la** cometa – kite, **la** coma – comma, **la** papa – potato, **la** capital – capital (city), etc.

Some nouns have ambiguous gender; some people use them as masculine and others as feminine.

> *Ej.* el/la azúcar, el/la mar, el/la sartén, el/la margen, el/la sauna, el/la radio, etc.

For some nouns that describe people, the difference in grammatical gender depends on the gender of the person. With professions traditionally reserved for men, the Spanish language hasn't fully caught up with the progressive shift in gender roles, leaving questions about the correct usage.

> *Ej.* el atleta (alto), el deportista (guapo), el modelo (viejo), el indígena, el psiquiatra, etc.
> la atleta (alta), la deportista (guapa), la modelo (vieja), la indígena, la psiquiatra, etc.
> Ella es el piloto? Ella es la piloto? Ella es la pilota? Ella es la juez? Ella es la jueza?

In the case of animal names, some have both masculine and feminine forms, based on the sex of the individual animal, and some are either masculine or feminine regardless of the animal's sex. In the latter cases, the words *macho* (male) and *hembra* (female) are used to distinguish its sex. Lastly, there are animals that have unique names for their respective sexes.

> *Ej.* el gato/la gata, el perro/la perra, el elefante/la elefanta, el león/la leona, etc.
> la jirafa (macho, hembra), el puma (macho, hembra), la ballena (macho, hembra), etc.
> el toro/la vaca, el gallo/la gallina, el tigre/la tigresa, el caballo/la yegua, etc.

88

Some nouns appear to break the rules because their colloquial (informal) form is actually short for a longer form, where the gender of the word is more obvious.

Ej. la foto(grafía), la moto(cicleta), la expo(sición), la disco(teca), etc.

The following nouns are feminine, but since they start with a *stressed* (tonic) *a*, the masculine article (definite – *el*/*la* or indefinite – *un*/*una*) is used. This is to avoid the double *a* sound, but, remember, only if the first syllable is stressed. Note that adjectives still agree with the gender of the noun, not the article. Also note that there is no double *a* problem if the noun is plural.

Ej. el/un alma (hermosa), el/un ave (muerta), el/un agua (fría), el/un área (pequeña), etc.
las almas (hermosas), unas aves (muertas), las aguas (frías), unas áreas (pequeñas), etc.

Lastly, the peculiar case of the word *arte*, whose singular form is masculine and plural form is feminine, as evidenced by the adjectives that modify them.

Ej. el arte romano, las bellas artes

- **Nouns and their number**

You've already seen the basic rules for making nouns plural from their singular form (p.7), but there are a few curious types of nouns that don't follow these rules. Take a look.

Ej. el robot/los robots (not robotes), el club/los clubs, el póster/los pósters, etc.

These words are taken directly from English and therefore usually use the plural form in English. The same is done in English with Spanish words: taco/tacos (not tacoes, like potatoes/tomatoes). Other plurals that are unique like their English counterparts are nouns ending in *is*. In these cases, the plural forms are the same as the singular forms. In English, the -is becomes -es.

Ej. la crisis → las crisis – crisis → crises, la tesis → las tesis – thesis → theses, etc.

There are other singular nouns ending in *s* that don't have separate plural forms (*el*/*los bíceps*, *virus, clímax, lunes, martes, miércoles, jueves, viernes*, etc.) and most compound nouns (*el*/*los abrelatas, paraguas, sacapuntas, sujetapapeles*, etc.). Many singular nouns that end in *í* or *ú* (with an accent mark) have two acceptable plural forms, one following the rules and one breaking them.

Ej. el colibrí → los colibríes/colibrís, el tabú → los tabúes/tabús, etc.

- **Adjectives also used as nouns**

You've learned about the nominalization (nouning) of adjectives (p.41), but some adjectives have been nominalized so frequently that they are now considered true nouns.

Ej. La chica (niña/muchacha) compró una camisa muy chica (pequeña).
El optimista tiene perspectivas optimistas.
La giganta vieja es más giganta que todos los demás gigantes.

- **Adjective placement**

You should know by now that adjectives most often follow the nouns they modify (p.7). This provides descriptive contrast.

> *Ej.* la casa <u>grande</u> (as opposed to the small house)
> los ojos <u>verdes</u> (as opposed to brown or blue eyes)

The purpose of adjectives, however, is not always to show contrast. This is the case of inherent characteristics. Often these characteristics are inherent to an individual or specific noun, or are inherent given a certain situation or circumstance. In these cases, the adjective comes first.

> *Ej.* las <u>grandes</u> Montañas Rocosas (there are no small Rocky Mountains)
> los <u>fríos</u> inviernos de Alaska (there are no warm Alaskan winters)
> los <u>verdes</u> ojos de mi hermano (he doesn't have any other color eyes)
> los <u>altos</u> rascacielos de Nueva York (all skyscrapers, by definition, are tall)

Other types of adjectives almost always precede the noun.

> ➢ Adjectives indicating quantity, specific or general
>   *Ej.* <u>docientas</u> personas, <u>muchos</u> problemas, <u>otra</u> cosa, <u>primera</u> vez, <u>tanta</u> gente
> ➢ Short-form possessive adjectives
>   *Ej.* <u>nuestras</u> amigas, <u>tu</u> bici, <u>sus</u> mascotas
> ➢ mejor, peor, más, menos (with quantities, *más* and *menos* usually come after)
>   *Ej.* tu <u>mejor</u> amigo, su <u>peor</u> pesadilla, <u>menos</u> tiempo, <u>más</u> tacos, (tres tacos <u>más</u>)

Some adjectives have a different meaning based on where they are placed.

> *Ej.* carro <u>nuevo</u> (latest model), <u>nuevo</u> carro (new to the owner, synonymous with *otro*)
> color <u>diferente</u> (unusual: chartreuse), <u>diferente</u> color (synonymous with *otro*)
> amigo <u>viejo</u> (refers to friend's age), <u>viejo</u> amigo (refers to the age of the friendship)
> <u>pura</u> agua (only water), agua <u>pura</u> (free of contaminants)
> la <u>misma</u> presidenta (the same as before), la presidenta <u>misma</u> (the president herself)

- **A word (or several) about *mismo***

The word *mismo* means "same" in some contexts, but it is also used to add emphasis either in examples like the one above or in reflexive like constructions meaning "oneself."

> *Ej.* Mario me dio regalos a mí. (*a mí* adds emphasis)
> Yo me di regalos a mí <u>mismo</u>. (*mismo* is added when the verb is reflexive)

¡Ojo! Above, *mism<u>o</u>* is masculine. This means that the person speaking is masculine. If the person speaking were female, *mism<u>a</u>* would be used. For plural pronouns, use *mism<u>os/as</u>*.

> *Ej.* Yo me di regalos a mí <u>misma</u>. (female speaking)
> Marta y yo nos dimos regalos a nosotras <u>mismas</u>. (Marta and speaker are both female)

o **Common *mismo* pitfall**

Many English speakers try to translate "myself" as "my" – *mi* "self" – *mismo* as though *mismo* were a noun to be possessed. In the previous example, *mí* has an accent mark, which means it is a pronoun, and *mismo* is an adjective modifying that pronoun, not the other way around. So, "ourselves" would be <u>*nosotros mismos*</u>, not <u>*nuestros mismos*</u>.

Indirect-object pronouns:	**Reflexive pronouns:**
me (a mí)	me (a mí mismo/a)
te (a ti)	te (a ti mismo/a)
le (a él/ella/Ud.)	se (a sí mismo/a)
nos (a nosotros/as)	nos (a nosotros/as mismos/as)
os (a vosotros/as)	os (a vosotros/as mismos/as)
les (a ellos/ellas/Uds.)	se (a sí mismos/as)

Ej. Mario nos dio regalos a mí y a mis hermanos. (he gave us)
Mario se dio regalos a sí mismo. (he gave himself)
Nosotros nos dimos regalos los unos a los otros. (we gave each other)
Nosotros nos dimos regalos a nosotros mismos. (we gave ourselves)

Now that you have a handle on reflexive pronouns, which use the preposition *a*, let's look at examples of prepositional phrases with a couple other prepositions. The same concepts apply.

conmigo (with me)	conmigo mismo/a (with myself)
contigo (with you)	contigo mismo/a (with yourself)
con él/ella/Ud. (with him/her/you)	consigo / con él/ella/Ud. mismo/a
con nosotros/as (with us)	con nosotros/as mismos/as (with ourselves)
con vosotros/as (with you)	con vosotros/as mismos/as (with yourselves)
con ellos/ellas/Uds. (with them/you)	consigo / con ellos/ellas/Uds. mismos/as

¡Ojo! Con is a unique preposition (*-migo, -tigo, -sigo*); all others follow the pattern below. Also, like the pronoun *yo*, *conmigo*, *contigo*, and *consigo* end in *o*, but are not masculine. There's no separate feminine *yo* (*ya?*); there's no *conmig<u>a</u>*, *contig<u>a</u>*, or *consig<u>a</u>*.

para mí (for me)	para mí mismo/a (for myself)
para ti (for you)	para ti mismo/a (for yourself)
para él/ella/Ud. (for him/her/you)	para sí mismo/a (for himself/herself/yourself)
para nosotros/as (for us)	para nosotros/as mismos/as (for ourselves)
para vosotros/as (for you)	para vosotros/as mismos/as (for yourselves)
para ellos/ellas/Uds. (for them/you)	para sí mismos/as (for themselves/yourselves)

The word *mismo* is not limited to object pronouns; it can be used to emphasize subjects, too.

Ej. Yo mismo/a voy a preparar la cena. (I myself ...)
Tú mismo/a puedes aprender español. (You yourself ...)
Mario mismo quiere hacerlo. (Mario himself ...)
Ellas mismas dieron la fiesta. (They themselves ...)

- **Adjectives also used as adverbs**

Adjectives modify nouns and, in Spanish, agree with them in gender and number. Adverbs, on the other hand, modify verbs, adjectives, and other adverbs, and have no agreement with anything. Hopefully these concepts are not foreign to you any more, but there are always difficult cases. Navigating adverbs that double as adjectives, especially when modifying an adjective, is not exactly intuitive. Here are some of these adjectives, in their adjective forms.

> *Ej.* medio litro – half a liter   demasiado tiempo – too much time
> media hora – half an hour   demasiadas casas – too many houses
> pocos cambios – few changes   bastante viento – quite a bit of wind
> poca comida – little (not much) food   bastantes herramientas – enough tools

The masculine, singular forms of the adjectives above double as adverbs. Remember, regardless of the noun being modified, adverbs do not modify nouns, so gender and number are nonexistent.

> *Ej.* Los muchachos son *demasiado* perezosos. – The youngsters are *too* lazy.
> La gente está *demasiado* enojada. – The people are *too* angry.
> Nosotros estamos *medio* locos. – We are *kind of* crazy.
> Ellas son *medio* hermanas. – They are *half* sisters.
> Los panes son *poco* saludables. – Breads are *not very* healthful.
> La casa está *un poco* sucia. – The house is *a bit* dirty.
> Juanita es *bastante* talentosa. – She is *quite* talented.
> Mis tíos son *bastante* viejos. – My aunt and uncle are *quite* old.

- **Consecutive adjectives and adverbs**

In Spanish, you can use multiple adjectives to describe the same noun or string multiple adverbs together. In the case of adjectives, when not specifically distinguishing between two or more similar objects, you use *y* to separate the last two adjectives, and commas to separate the rest.

> *Ej.* La casa es grande, lujosa y muy cara.
> Los empleados son honestos y sinceros.

When specifically distinguishing between two or more similar objects, you may eliminate the commas and the *y*, the first adjectives being the ones the objects have in common and the last ones being the ones that differentiate them. In most cases, you'll limit it to two adjectives.

> *Ej.* No me gusta la casa grande amarilla, sino la casa grande blanca.

Stringing multiple adverbs together is fairly intuitive. Remember, you can add *-mente* to the end of the feminine, singular form of many adjectives to make them adverbs (p.18). If you have consecutive adverbs with the ending *-mente*, reserve the *-mente* for the final adverb.

> *Ej.* El candidato habla *bien mal.* (muy mal)
> ¡Los novios están *completamente* y *locamente* enamorados!
> Los socios presentaron el presupuesto *clara, concisa* y *eficazmente.*

- **Diminutives, superlatives, and other fun effects**

There are three common suffixes to form the diminutive of a word: -ito/a, -illo/a, and -ico/a. The difference between these suffixes is mostly regional, but -ito/a is the most universal. The purpose of a diminutive form is to describe something physically smaller than one might expect, make something seem less imposing or less direct, and/or to make something sound cute.

Ej. la mesa – the table   la mes<u>ita</u> – the little table
                                       la mes<u>ica</u> – the little table

     una pregunta – a question   una pregunt<u>ita</u> – a quick question
                                       una pregunt<u>illa</u> – a quick question

     los gatos – the cats   los gat<u>itos</u> – the kittens / the tiny cats

     Miguel – Michael   Miguel<u>ito</u> – Mikey

Sometimes the suffix requires a *c*, which makes it easier to pronounce, but the rules governing this are speculative and are not universal; some people may use the *c*, whereas others may not.

Ej. un caf<u>é</u> – a coffee   un cafe<u>cito</u> – a cup of coffee

     un pueblo – a town   un puebl<u>ito</u> – a small town
                                       un pueble<u>cito</u> – a small town

     una vieja – an old woman   una viej<u>ita</u> – a little old lady
                                       una vieje<u>cita</u> – a little old lady

     pobre – poor   pobre<u>cito</u> – (you) poor thing
                                       pobre<u>cillo</u> – (you) poor thing

     un favor – a favor   un favor<u>cito</u> – a small favor

Diminutives are not limited to nouns; they can be adjectives or adverbs as well.

Ej. por favor – please   por favor<u>cito</u> – pretty please

     perdón – I'm sorry   perdon<u>cito</u> – I'm so sorry

     más o menos – okay / fine   más o men<u>itos</u> – okay / fine (cuter)

     adiós – bye   adios<u>ito</u> – bye bye

     pequeña – small   pequeñ<u>ita</u> – really small

     gordo – fat   gord<u>ito</u> – "kinda" fat / a "li'l fatty"

The smaller and cuter and less direct you want to be, the more -*it*'s you can add; there's no limit.

Ej. chiqu<u>itas</u> – really small   chiqu<u>ititas</u> – really super small

     rapid<u>ito</u> – really quickly   rapid<u>itito</u> – really really quickly

     un bes<u>ito</u> – a little kiss   un bes<u>itito</u> – a li'l itty bitty kiss

A few diminutives are formed with *i*.

Ej. mamá → mami, papá → papi, chulo/a → chuli, Yolanda → Yoli, etc.

¡Ojo! Some nouns look like diminutives, but they have their own separate meanings.

> *Ej.* manzana – apple   manzanilla – chamomile
> mesa – table   mesilla – nightstand

To have the opposite effect of the diminutive form, use the suffix *-ote/a*. This is called the augmentative and makes something seem bigger, more imposing, and/or more offensive. Notice the masculine form ends in *e*. For some words, adding *-ón* has this same effect.

> *Ej.* una palabra – a word   una palab<u>rota</u> – a swear word
> una gor<u>da</u> – a fat woman   una gor<u>dota</u> – a big ol' fat woman
> un abrazo – a hug   un abra<u>zote</u> – a giant hug
> un burrito – a burrito   un bur<u>rote</u> – a big burrito
> un favor – a favor   un favor<u>zote</u> – a huge favor
> un problema – a problem   un proble<u>món</u> – a big problem

The bigger, more imposing you want the word to be, the more *-ot*'s you can add.

> *Ej.* un burr<u>otote</u> – a big, fat burrito   un burr<u>ototote</u> – a big fat "honkin'" burrito
> grand<u>ota</u> – huge   grand<u>otota</u> – crazy huge
> un gat<u>ote</u> – a giant cat   un gat<u>otote</u> – an enormous cat

You can add these endings to adjectives and the nouns they modify for maximum effect. If you throw in the word *pero*, followed by a long pause, like you're struggling to believe it yourself, it's like saying, "and I mean *really* …"

> *Ej.* una casita pequeñita – a teeny, tiny house
> Es una casita, pero pequeñita. – It's a tiny house, and I mean *really* tiny.
> Es fuerte, ¡pero fuertote! – He's strong, and I mean *really* strong!

The prefix *requete-* or *re-*, for short, adds intensity to an adjective.

> *Ej.* ¡Ese gato es <u>requete</u>feo! – That cat is ugly as hell!
> Estaba <u>re</u>cansada cuando llegué a casa. – I was super tired when I got home.
> ¡Los modelos son <u>re</u>guapos! – The models are crazy good looking!

You've seen how to use one superlative form (p.61), but there is also a suffix that is considered another form of the superlative: *-ísimo/a*. Notice the accent mark on the antepenultimate (third-to-last) syllable. This superlative form is like adding "really" to an adjective.

> *Ej.* grande – big   grand<u>ísimo</u>/a – really big
> buenas – good   buen<u>ísimas</u> – really good

As you might suspect, you can add "really" as many times as you want by adding more and more *is*'s. Feel free to go wild with this for comical effect, but remember your accent mark on the antepenultimate syllable.

> *Ej.* famos<u>ísima</u> – really famous   famos<u>isisísima</u> – really, really, really famous
> tont<u>ísimo</u> – really stupid   tont<u>isísimo</u> – really, really stupid

Ser vs. estar

You've been working with *ser* and *estar* since the first couple units (pp.9, 23). You've seen several rules and many more examples, yet there is still more to understand. Both mean "to be," yet they are not interchangeable (of course there are a few exceptions). Let's review and expand.

- **Use *ser:***

  - to describe origin. (<u>Soy</u> de Nevada.)
  - to describe physical characteristics. (El carro <u>era</u> verde.)
  - to describe time. (<u>Eran</u> las 11:30 de la noche.)
  - to describe days. (Ayer <u>fue</u> jueves.)
  - to describe dates. (Mi cumpleaños <u>es</u> el 1 de abril.)
  - to describe character traits. (Alejandro <u>es</u> inteligente.)
  - to describe professions. (Itzel siempre <u>ha sido</u> profesora.)
  - to describe relationships. (Ellas <u>son</u> medio hermanas.)
  - to describe what something is made of. (El anillo <u>es</u> de platino.)
  - to describe events in the passive voice. (La casa <u>fue</u> destruida por la tormenta.)
  - to describe when or where an event takes place. (La fiesta <u>será</u> en mi casa.)

- **Use *estar*:**

  - to describe physical location. (<u>Estamos</u> en Colorado.)
  - to describe physical position. (<u>Estuvieron</u> acostadas.)
  - to describe ongoing action. (<u>Estaba</u> corriendo.)
  - to describe mental states of being. (<u>Estamos</u> locas.)
  - to describe emotional states of being. (<u>Estaban</u> deprimidos.)
  - to describe physical states of being. (La comida <u>está</u> caliente.)
  - to describe the result of an action. (La casa <u>está</u> destruida gracias al tornado.)
  - to describe what something is made of. (El rascacielos <u>está</u> *hecho* de acero y cemento.)
  - to describe what something looks like. (<u>Estás</u> guapa hoy.)
  - to describe a characteristic in contrast to expectations. (¡Guau, qué alto <u>está</u> tu hijo!)
  - to describe a temporary job. (Manuel <u>está</u> *de* mesero.)

¡Ojo! Thinking *ser* is permanent and *estar* is temporary is an oversimplified approach to understanding this breakdown that will lead you astray.

> *Ej.* Mi abuelo <u>está</u> muerto. (and not coming back) La casa <u>es</u> azul. (but could be painted)

Many adjectives change meaning depending on whether *ser* or *estar* is used. Here are a few.

	ser – to be	estar – to be
libre	free (a right / not jailed)	free (not busy or occupied)
aburrido/a	boring	bored
entretenido/a	entertaining	entertained
cansado/a	tiring	tired (worn out)
molesto/a	annoying (*molestoso*)	annoyed
vivo/a	a living being	alive
rico/a	rich (not poor)	delicious (food or experience, etc.)
verde	green	unripe
bueno/a	good	good (food – tasty, person – good looking)
malo/a	bad	sick
preparado/a	educated (schooling)	prepared (ready)
listo/a	clever / witty / smart	ready
seguro/a	safe (not dangerous)	sure / certain (person), safe (not in danger)
orgulloso/a	prideful	proud
loco/a	scatter-brained	crazy
atento/a	attentive / courteous	aware
consciente	conscientious	awake / conscious (not unconscious)

The following are a few adjectives that permit *ser* or *estar* without changing meanings.

> *Ej.* casado/a, soltero/a, viudo/a, ciego/a, manco/a, sordo/a,
> cojo/a (ser/estar cojo – disability, estar cojo – injury)

Haber – To Be (sort of)

You've been studying *haber* as an auxiliary (helping) verb in perfect tenses, but you first saw it in a completely different contex (p.21). Although it is the same verb in both cases, for all intents and purposes, it is different.

¡Ojo! In the following contexts, *haber* has no subject, therefore there is only one conjugation per tense. The thing that *is* is the direct object. Think of it as *tener*, without a subject.

> *Ej.* ¿Por qué buscar <u>problemas</u> donde no <u>los</u> hay? (hay/tengo una cosa – la hay / la tengo)

Indicativo:

presente – hay (there is/are)
pretérito – hubo (there was/were)
imperfect – había (there was/were, there used to be)
futuro – habrá (there will be)
condicional – habría (there would be)
presente perfecto – ha habido (there has/have been)
pluscuamperfecto – había habido (there had been)
futuro perfecto – habrá habido (there will have been)
condicional perfecto – habría habido (there would have been)

Subjuntivo:

presente – que haya (that there be)

imperfecto – que hubiera (that there be)

presente perfecto – que haya habido
pluscuamperfecto – que hubiera habido

Lo de "lo" – The Thing About "lo"

The word *lo* has multiple uses. You know it best as a direct-object pronoun and you may remember it as what some call the neuter form (p.61). There is another way you have used it hundreds of times by now, but probably don't fully grasp why. I'm referring to *lo siento*. This *lo* is an anaphoric reference, which is a word that refers to an idea previously stated in the conversation.

> *Ej.* Eugenio: <u>Mi gato ha muerto hoy</u>.
> Carmen: ¡Ay, no! <u>Lo</u> siento mucho.

- **Common *lo siento* pitfall**

The *lo* of *lo siento* refers to whatever was mentioned that you feel bad for, so if Carmen in the above example found out from someone else that Eugenio's cat had died, she wouldn't call up Eugenio out of the blue and say, "*Lo siento mucho.*" She would need to specify what she felt bad about, and she couldn't use *lo* ("<u>*Lo siento mucho que tu gato haya muerto.*</u>") because the cat's death would have not yet been mentioned in that conversation. Carmen, therefore, would say, "*Siento mucho que tu gato haya muerto.*"

The anaphoric *lo* is also commonly used with the verbs *ser* and *estar*. Notice that, in English, no word is necessary; the concept is simply omitted.

> *Ej.* Marta: Pepa, ¡eres <u>maleducada y molestosa</u>!
> Pepa: ¡No <u>lo</u> soy; <u>lo</u> eres tú! – No I'm not; you are!
>
> Arturo: ¿<u>Lista</u>, María?
> María: Sí, <u>lo</u> estoy. – Yes, I am (ready).

Knowing that the meanings of some adjectives depend on whether you use *ser* or *estar*, you could have some fun with the last example. The joke would be on the person who asked the question without specifying the intended (assumed) verb.

> *Ej.* Arturo: ¿<u>Lista</u>, María?
> María: Sí, <u>lo</u> *soy*. – Yes, I am *witty*.

Saber is another verb that, in theory, requires an anaphoric *lo*, but it is frequently omitted.

> *Ej.* Rigoberto: ¿<u>A qué hora empieza el partido</u>?
> Catrina: No <u>lo</u> sé. (No sé.) – I don't know.

¡Ojo! The anaphoric *lo* has no gender or number as it is not a direct-object pronoun; it's always *lo*.

The *lo* in phrases like *lo chistoso es* (p.61) is, for all intents and purposes, the same as the anaphoric *lo*, but there needn't be any previous idea stated in that very conversation. Like in the title of this lesson, "*lo de*" is a very common phrase and means "the thing" or "the thing about."

> *Ej.* Estoy pensando en <u>lo de</u> ayer. No te preocupes de <u>lo de</u> tu jefe.

Unidad 30

La acentuación y la entonación – Accentuation and Intonation

➢ If the word **ends** in a **vowel, *n*, or *s*,** the stressed syllable (*sílaba tónica*) is the second-to-last. All other syllables in the word are unstressed (*sílabas átonas*).

ca<u>mi</u>na	
<u>co</u>rre	*palabras **llanas*** – words stressed on the **penultimate** syllable
ca<u>mi</u>nan	
<u>co</u>rres	no accent mark needed
calce<u>ti</u>nes	
vis<u>tien</u>do	
entrena<u>do</u>ra	

➢ If the word **ends** in **any other consonant**, the stressed syllable (*sílaba tónica*) is the last. All other syllables in the word are unstressed (*sílabas átonas*).

cami<u>nar</u>	
pa<u>red</u>	*palabras **agudas*** – words stressed on the **final** syllable
entrena<u>dor</u>	
su<u>til</u>	no accent mark needed

➢ If the word does not follow the first two rules, a written accent mark is needed to show which syllable is stressed (sílaba tónica).

<u>lá</u>piz	*palabra llana*: penultimate syllable stressed with accent mark; breaks 2nd rule
<u>cés</u>ped	*palabra llana*: penultimate syllable stressed with accent mark; breaks 2nd rule
televi<u>sión</u>	*palabra aguda*: final syllable stressed with accent mark; breaks 1st rule
so<u>fá</u>	*palabra aguda*: final syllable stressed with accent mark; breaks 1st rule
calce<u>tín</u>	*palabra aguda*: final syllable stressed with accent mark; breaks 1st rule
vis<u>tién</u>dome	*palabra **esdrújula***: antepenultimate syllable stressed w/accent mark; breaks 1st rule
<u>ú</u>til	*palabra llana*: penultimate syllable stressed with accent mark; breaks 2nd rule
cami<u>ná</u>bamos	*palabra **esdrújula***: antepenultimate syllable stressed w/accent mark; breaks 1st rule

las vocales fuertes/abiertas (strong/open vowels): **a, e, o, á, é, í, ó, ú**

las vocales débiles/cerradas (weak/closed vowels): **i, u, ü**

diptongo (two vowels pronounced in one syllable): vocal fuerte + vocal débil
vocal débil + vocal débil

caigo	**sei**s	c**iu**dad	contin**uo**	g**ua**nte	**cau**sar
c**ie**ncia	d**eu**da	c**ui**dado	per**ió**dico	**ahu**mado (the *h* is not a factor)

el hiato/adiptongo (two vowels pronounced in different syllables): vocal fuerte + vocal fuerte

ca**er**	v**eo**	te**ní**amos	contin**úo**	c**ao**s	**oa**sis
oc**éa**no	**oe**ste	ca**í**da	le**í**do	almo**hoa**da (the *h* is not a factor)

el triptongo (three vowels pronounced in a single syllable): vocal fuerte + dos vocales débiles

averig**üéi**s	**guau**	limp**iau**ñas	sem**iau**tomático

- **Common intonation pitfalls**

When it comes to cognates or words that share their roots with a word in English, a common mistake is to stress the syllable that is stressed in the English word instead of following the rules.

Ej. ¿Qué sig·ni·fi·ca?   vs.   sig·ni·fi·cance → ¿Qué sig·~~ni~~·fi·ca?

Yo par·ti·ci·po …   vs.   par·ti·ci·pate   → Yo par·~~ti~~·ci·po …

Tú co·or·di·nas …   vs.   co·or·di·nate   → Tú co·~~or~~·di·nas …

In any given word, there can only be one tonic (stressed) syllable, the rest are atonic (unstressed). Adverbs with the suffix *-mente* are the unofficial exception to the rule. The syllable that would be stressed in the adjective form, before adding the suffix *-mente*, stays stressed and the penultimate (second-to-last) syllable of *-mente* is also stressed, following the rules on the previous page. If the adjective form has an accent mark, the corresponding adverb form retains that accent mark.

Ej. pro·ba·ble → pro·ba·ble·men·te

rá·pi·da   → rá·pi·da·men·te

fre·cuen·te → fre·cuen·te·men·te

Be careful not to assume the stressed and unstressed syllables alternate rhythmically. The following examples have back-to-back stressed syllables.

Ej. nor·mal → nor·mal·men·te (~~nor~~·mal·men·te)

co·mún → co·mún·men·te (~~co~~·mun·men·te)

A *clitic* is a single-syllable, unstressed word that is intonated as though it were attached to the word that either precedes it or follows it. This sounds ridiculous in English as we are accustomed to stressing any word or syllable that we want to add emphasis to. Spanish does not allow such freedom.

Ej. Mi ca·sa es su ca·sa. – In this common phrase, only the *ca* is stressed. Fight the urge to stress the contrast between possessive adjectives, "~~Mi~~ casa es ~~su~~ casa."

¿Pre·fie·res tu ca·fé con le·che o sin le·che? – I know you want to stress *con* and *sin*, as you probably did just now in your head, but native speakers would not stress these clitics in Spanish.

There is no hard and fast rule that I have ever come across for this, so you must listen intently to native Spanish speakers from around the world if you want to master this native intonation.

Ej. ¿Es pa·ra mí o pa·ra ti? – In this case, you should stress the *mí* and the *ti*.

Yo no lo quie·ro. – The *yo* could be stressed here, or not.

No lo quie·ro yo. – *Yo*, here, is placed at the end to be emphasized.

La pronunciación

As you can imagine, it's tough to teach pronunciation on paper. In the first unit (p.6), I gave you some rough basics to get you started, but mastery can only come through listening. Every country or region has a unique dialect, including pronunciation of certain letters. The biggest difference between accents in English is the way people pronounce vowels. In Spanish, vowel sounds are universal, but some consonants vary quite a bit. If you study phonetics in Spanish, you'll learn that some consonants have several unique sounds, like *n*, depending on the letters on either side of them. It isn't necessary—or practical—for the average person to learn phonetics to master pronunciation, so here are some advanced observations you can try to tune your ear to when listening to native speakers.

➤ There is no *schwa* /ə/ sound in Spanish. When pronouncing your vowels, try to open your mouth to an exaggerated, almost comical extent. This will keep *schwa* at bay.
  Ej. el<u>e</u>ph<u>a</u>nt (the underlined vowels here are the *schwa* sound in English, like "uh")
  <u>e</u>l<u>e</u>fant<u>e</u> (all three sound the same, like *ten* in Spanish)

➤ Vowels have only one sound each in Spanish.
  Ej. *a* is always *a* as in <u>agua</u>
  e is always *e* as in <u>eres</u> (*tres* and *seis* do not rhyme)
  i is always *i* as in *mi* (*idea* is a tricky one; give it a shot)
  o is always *o* as in <u>tomo</u>
  u is always *u* as in <u>uno</u> (never "yu" like "<u>u</u>se" in English)

➤ The *h* is silent, except in foreign words (*hockey*, *sushi*) and when preceded by *c* (*ch*). Pronounce words with *h* as though the *h* weren't there at all.
  Ej. "onor" (<u>h</u>onor), "carboidrato" (carbo<u>h</u>idrato), "desacer" (des<u>h</u>acer), etc.

➤ The *ch* sound in Spanish is almost universally like the "ch" sound in English in the word "change," but in northern Mexico, the *ch* sound is more like the "sh" sound in the English word "<u>sh</u>elf." "*Son las o<u>sh</u>o de la no<u>sh</u>e.*" In Spain and Chile, there's a subtle "ts" sound to it.

➤ The *k* sound in *co, ca, cu, que,* and *qui,* is much softer than it is in English. It borders on an English "g" sound.

➤ The soft *g* sound and the *j* sound are identical to each other in Spanish, but there is quite a difference between countries in how harsh of a sound it makes. In Mexico, for example, it is very soft, like an English "h" in the word "hope." In Spain, on the other hand, it has a very harsh, scratchy, throaty sound.

➤ The hard *g* sound in Spanish ranges from a little more subtle than the English "g" sound to an almost silent sound, particularly when followed by *u*.

➤ The *y* and the *ll* sounds are identical to each other in many countries and range in sound from the English "y" in "yoyo," like in Mexico, to the English "j" in Joe, like in Colombia, and even the French "g" like in the word *bourgeoise*, like in Argentina. Some countries, however, distinguish between the two, like in Paraguay, where the *y* is like the Mexican *y* but the *ll* is pronounced like *ly* – "calye" (*calle*).

➢ The *t* in Spanish is much softer than the "t" in English.

➢ The *d* is also much softer, close to the "th" in the English "those."

➢ The *b* and *v* sounds in Spanish are identical to each other. The possible confusion leads people to give them nicknames "*b grande*" or "*b alta*" because it is the largest/tallest of the two, and "*v chica*" or "*v corta*" because it is the smallest/shortest of the two. Some even say, "*b de burro*" o "*v de vaca*." Their sound varies by dialect, but often lies somewhere between the "b" and "v" in English.

➢ The *p* so soft that it is often mistaken for *b* by native English speakers. A deliberate ear and increased literacy will help resolve this issue.

➢ The letter *n* in Spanish has at least six different pronunciations. The easiest one to teach on paper is the *m* sound it makes when followed by *p*, *b/v*, or *m*.
   Ej. "um poco" (un poco), "um bistec" (un bistec), "emviar" (enviar)

➢ The phonetic symbol *theta* /θ/ represents the *z* and soft *c* sounds. In central and northern Spain, these letters sound like the "th" in the English word "think." In southern Spain and the rest of the Spanish-speaking world, *z* and *c* are pronounced like *s*, which is known as "*el seseo.*"
   Ej. "diethiséis" vs. "diesiséis" (dieciséis), "thapatos" vs. "sapatos" (zapatos)

➢ The letter *x* most often sounds like *ks*, – "*ekstra*" (extra), but in parts of Spain it sounds like *s* – "*estra*" (extra). In indigenous words in Mexico, it has an *s* sound (Xochimilco), a *j* sound (México), or an English "sh" sound (mexica).

➢ The *s* in Spain has a very soft hissing quality to it, whereas in Latin America, it is pronounced like an English "s." The exception to this is when it's followed by *b/v*, *d*, *g*, *m,* or *n*. In these cases, you may detect a subtle English "z" quality to it.
   Ej. "dezde" (desde), "muzgo" (musgo), "ezmeralda" (esmeralda)

➢ The non-rolling *r* sound is very similar to the English "d" sound. This non-rolling *r* is only found directly between vowels within the same word.
   Ej. pero, cara, güero, ira, gurú, para, arena, aro, etc.

➢ The rolling *r* sound comes from a double *r (rr)* between vowels, or a single *r* not between two vowels of the same word. The action of rolling the *r* is "*ronronear.*"
   Ej. perro, carro, guerra, Raúl, risa, contra, enrollamos, lacra, coordina, etc.

If the *r* is at the end of a word, it rolls, but without voice, whispered, like a cat's purr.
   Ej. bailar, escoger, salir, por, flor, etc.

➢ The *words **y*** and ***o*** become *e* and ***u*** when followed by *i* and *o* sounds respectively. These are formal, written changes but stem from pronunciation issues.
   Ej. español y̶ **e** i̲nglés, oxígeno y̶ **e** h̲idrógeno
        uno o̶ **u** o̲tro, siete o̶ **u** o̲cho, adiós o̶ **u** h̲ola

Remember that *c* and *g* have hard and soft sounds and that *z*, *qu* and *j* share phonetic spellings with them respectively (p.34). Adding *u* or *ü* to *g* rounds out the list.

> *Ej.* ga (ponga), go (digo), gu (gurú), gue (guerra), gui (guía)
> gua (agua), guo (contiguo), ~~guu~~, güe (bilingüe), güi (pingüino)
> ja (naranja), jo (José), ju (jugo), ge (general) / je (jerarquía), gi (gigante) / ji (jirafa)
> ca (casa), co (color), cu (culebra), que (queso), qui (quiero)
> cua (cualidad), cuo (inocuo), ~~cuu~~, cue (cuero), cui (cuidado)
> za (zapato), zo (comienzo), zu (azúcar), ce (celebrar), ci (cierro)

In just about every case, the goal is to maintain the same sound, not the same letter, when going back and forth from one form of a word to another.

> *Ej.* jue<u>go</u> → jue<u>gue</u>   averi<u>gua</u> → averi<u>güe</u>
> esco<u>ge</u> → esco<u>jo</u>   alo<u>ja</u> → alo<u>je</u> (no reason to change to *g*)
> ata<u>ca</u> → ata<u>que</u>   Puerto Ri<u>co</u> → puertorri<u>que</u>ño
> ven<u>ce</u> → ven<u>zo</u>   comien<u>za</u> → comien<u>ces</u> (see note below about *ze*)

¡Ojo! Ze and *zi* are used in foreign words and archaic spellings (*zigzaguear, zebra, enzima,* etc.).

El alfabeto / el abecedario

There are 27 letters in the Spanish alphabet: the 26 English letters and *ñ*; *k* and *w* are used only for foreign words (*kilo, whisky,* etc.). There used to be 30, but *ch, ll,* and *rr* were eliminated in 1994. The only impact this change had on the language was alphabetical order (*cara, chino, coche* was *cara, coche, chino*). Unnecessary accent marks on monosyllabic words were also eliminated at the same time (*sóis, váis, véis, dáis, vé, fué, fuí, ví, vió, dí, dió, ó,* etc.) These changes were made to simplify the language. Note: *sé, él, tú, sí, té, dé, más,* etc. kept their accent marks for contrast with other words: *se, el, tu, si, te, de, mas,* etc.

a – *a*	**ñ** – *eñe*	**á** – *a con acento*
b – *be*	**o** – *o*	**é** – *e con acento*
c – *ce*	**p** – *pe*	**í** – *i con acento*
d – *de*	**q** – *cu*	**ó** – *o con acento*
e – *e*	**r** – *ere / erre*	**ú** – *u con acento*
f – *efe*	**s** – *ese*	
g – *ge*	**t** – *te*	**ü** – *u con crema* (or *con diéresis*)
h – *hache*	**u** – *u*	
i – *i* (*latina / romana*)	**v** – *ve / uve* (España)	
j – *jota*	**w** – *doble ve / ve doble / uve doble* (España) / *doble u*	
k – *ka*	**x** – *equis*	
l – *ele*	**y** – *i griega / ye*	**ch** – *ce hache* (formerly *che*)
m – *eme*	**z** – *zeta*	**ll** – *doble ele* (formerly *elle*)
n – *ene*		**rr** – *doble ere* (formerly *erre*)

la letra – letter	la sílaba – syllable	la palabra – word
la vocal – vowel	la hache – the letter h	la letra minúscula – lowercase letter
la consonante – consonant	la jota – the letter j	la letra mayúscula – capital letter

Irregular Conjugations That Stem From Pronunciation Issues

You've seen some irregular gerund forms (p.47) that require a *y* to break up the otherwise weak pronunciation of *aiendo* and *eiendo*. This (*i → y*) change makes these words easier to pronounce.

Ej. traer → trayendo, leer → leyendo, ir → yendo, etc.

Although some words, like *compañía*, have ñ followed by *í* (*i* with accent mark) and a vowel, verbs ending in *ñir* lose their *i* (*i* without accent mark) for the preterite *ió/ieron*, the gerund *iendo*, and the imperfect subjunctive *iera, ieras, iéramos*, etc. to avoid the weak pronunciation of ñ followed by *i* (*i* without accent mark) and a vowel.

teñir (e → i) – to dye

preterite

teñí	teñimos
teñiste	teñisteis
tiñó	tiñeron

gerund

tiñendo

imperfect subjunctive

tiñera	tiñéramos
tiñeras	tiñerais
tiñera	tiñeran

gruñir – to grunt / to growl

preterite

gruñí	gruñimos
gruñiste	gruñisteis
gruñó	gruñeron

gerund

gruñendo

imperfect subjunctive (alternate)

gruñese	gruñésemos
gruñeses	gruñeseis
gruñese	gruñesen

The verb *yacer* has three acceptable conjugations for the *yo* form: *yazco, yazgo, yago* due to pronunciation doubts. The verb *erguir* has two acceptable conjugations for the same reason.

erguir (e → i) – to straighten up / to put upright

present indicative

yergo / irgo	erguimos
yergues / irgues	erguís
yergue / irgue	yerguen / irguen

present subjunctive

yerga / irga	yergamos / irgamos
yergas / irgas	yergáis / irgáis
yerga / irga	yergan / irgan

The **imperative** follows the same patterns above. See p.109 for more on *nosotros* and *vosotros*.

(+) yo: ------------
(–) yo: ------------

(+) tú: yergue / irgue
(–) tú: no yergas / irgas

(+) Ud.:   yerga / irga
(–) Ud.: no yerga / irga

(+) nosotros: yergamos / irgamos (basically subjunctive)
(–) nosotros: no yergamos / irgamos (basically subjunctive)

(+) vosotros: erguid (as with *tú*, not simply subjunctive)
(–) vosotros: no yergáis / irgáis (basically subjunctive)

(+) Uds.:   yergan / irgan
(–) Uds.: no yergan / irgan

Querid@ estudiante,

   ¡Felicidades! ¡Lo has hecho: has cumplido con todo y lo sabes todo! Ahora, eres capaz de hablar de cualquier tema de interés, sin error alguno ni malentendido, con todos los hablantes nativos de español de todo el mundo, incluso a pesar de la jerga, de su acento, de su formación, y de las expresiones idiomáticas que usen de todas las épocas de la historia del mundo.

   ¡No te creas! Apenas has comenzado. Ahora tienes la base para seguir aprendiendo sin guía. Has leído mucho y has aprendido un montón, la verdad, pero siempre habrá más para aprender. Siempre. Es imposible poner todo lo que haya para aprender en un solo libro. Te dejo con unas últimas lecciones a continuación, pero sigue repasando todas las lecciones y listas de vocabulario de este libro mismo. El resto es responsabilidad tuya. Échale ganas al mundo. Viaja. Explora el idioma. Ve a conocer mucha gente. Toma más clases de español. Lee revistas en español, escucha la radio en español, estudia la música en español, mira la tele y muchas películas en español, escribe en español, lee literatura y poesía en español y aun piensa en español. Nunca dejes de avanzar porque todo lo que has adquirido se te puede perder. No te olvides: allá donde fueres, haz lo que vieres.

Abrazotes,

David

Unidad X

Los múltiples usos del "se"

The pronoun *se* may not seem complicated, but it is one of the most versatile words in the Spanish language and, therefore, one of the most difficult to master. You've seen it many times over as a reflexive pronoun (pp.25-27, 36-38), often translated as "oneself" (*llamarse, acostarse*) but frequently impossible to translate (*morirse, reírse*), but that's just one of its uses. In addition to the <u>reflexive</u> *se*, there is also the <u>passive</u> *se* and the <u>impersonal</u> *se*.

- **El "se" pasivo y la voz pasiva (ser + participio pasado)**

You've seen the past participle as an adjective (pp.62-63) but, so far, only with the verb *estar* to show a state of being or the result of an action. With few exceptions, the same past participle can also be used with the verb *ser*, but, in this context, it creates a passive voice for the action itself. The passive voice is a way of describing an action without needing to reference—or even know— the one who did the action. In the passive voice, the subject of the verb is what would otherwise be the direct object of the active voice.

> *Ej.* The house was built in 1964. (passive voice)
> My dad built the house in 1964. (active voice)

In the passive voice, the house is the subject; in the active voice, the house is the direct object.

> *Ej.* La casa fue construida en 1964. (voz pasiva)
> Mi papá construyó la casa en 1964. (voz activa)

It's important to note that the past participle (adjective) must agree with the subject in gender and number and the verb *ser* must be conjugated, likewise, according to that subject. If you do want to reference the person/thing responsible for the action, use *por* (by).

> *Ej.* Nosotras <u>fuimos</u> lesiona<u>das</u> anoche *por* el granizo.
> <u>Los</u> idiomas <u>han</u> sido estudiad<u>os</u> *por* los lingüistas durante siglos.

The passive *se* can often be substituted for the passive construction above but not in every case, and you cannot assign responsibility with the passive *se* due to the nature of its agreement with the subject. Although it isn't reflexive semantically, grammatically it acts as though it were. As with the reflexive *se*, the passive *se* encompasses all six pronouns: *me, te, se, nos, os, se*.

> *Ej.* Nosotras nos lesionamos anoche.
> (~~We injured ourselves last night.~~ We were injured last night.)
>
> Los idiomas se han estudiado durante siglos.
> (~~Languages have studied themselves ....~~ Languages have been studied for centuries.)

- **El "se" impersonal**

Surely you've asked, "*¿Cómo se dice …?*" and seen a sign that says, "*Se habla español.*" Are you asking how something says itself? Does the sign mean that Spanish speaks itself? Of course not, so the use of *se* in these examples is certainly not reflexive. Do they mean that something gets said or that Spanish gets spoken? Perhaps. Prescriptive linguists (those whose mission it is to tell people how to speak) might argue that the impersonal *se* doesn't exist, that it is simply the passive *se*. Descriptive linguists (those whose mission is to describe how people speak) would argue that the impersonal *se* most definitely exists as evidenced by the verb's lack of agreement with the subject in signs around the Spanish-speaking world.

Signs like "*Se vende bicicletas*" and "*Se busca empleados*" are commonplace around the Spanish-speaking world. Could it be that all of them are grammatically incorrect because "*vende/bicicletas*" and "*busca/empleados*" don't agree? I'll let you decide.

If you don't accept the existence of the impersonal *se*, then you would argue that the signs *should* say "*Se venden bicicletas*" and "*Se buscan empleados*."

If you accept the existence of the impersonal *se* as grammatically correct simply because hundreds of millions of Spanish speakers couldn't all be wrong, then let's simply describe it.

If you substitute *se* with *uno*, you get:

"~~Se~~ Uno dice …"	"~~Se~~ Uno habla español"
"~~Se~~ Uno vende bicicletas"	"~~Se~~ Uno busca empleados"

Boom! Now there's no problem grammatically because *uno* is your subject and all your verbs are 3rd person, singular. So there you have it: the impersonal *se* is a 3rd person, singular subject that means *uno*. We don't know who, but we do know it is some*one* impersonal.

Not so fast: does this answer hold up under scrutiny? Can we test it against any other grammatical conventions? What happens if we were to make these statements negative? Would our syntax (word order) hold up?

"*Uno no dice …*" → "*Se no dice …*" ??? Nope!
"*Uno no habla español*" → "*Se no habla español*" ??? No way!
"*Uno no vende bicicletas*" → "*Se no vende bicicletas*" ??? You're kidding, right?
"*Uno no busca empleados*" → "*Se no busca empleados*" ??? What?! NO!

And what happens if our verb is also reflexive? We obviously *have* to use *uno*, not *se*.

"*Cuando uno se levanta temprano …*" → "*Cuando se se levanta temprano …*" ??? 'fraid not!
"*Si uno se siente mal …*" → "*Si se se siente mal …*" ??? C'mon, stop messin' around!!

So, is the impersonal *se* just an internationally rampant grammatical error or a curious grammatical phenomenon? You're the expert now; it's time to decide for yourself!

- **Los accidentes – ¿culpable o víctima?**

In English, especially as children, we say things like, "it fell" and "it broke." Maybe the wind blew it over and it broke, but maybe it broke because I wasn't being careful with it. We turn the object into the subject to avoid blame, express that it was an accident, or illustrate that we were somehow the victim of the incident. This linguistic technique is much more common in Spanish than it is in English. The action verbs are reflexive and our part in it is as the indirect object (the victim of the accident). Common verbs include: olvidarse, caerse, perderse, romperse, ocurrirse, hacerse, and dificultarse. Don't forget R.I.D. (pp. 43, 53).

> *Ej.* El vaso se cayó. – The glass fell. (no one had anything to do with it)
> El vaso se me cayó. – I had something to do with its falling. Maybe I bumped it by accident or maybe it landed on me.
> Dejé caer el vaso. – I held it out and let it go on purpose.
>
> Las ventanas se rompieron. – The windows broke (got broken).
> Las ventanas se le rompieron a Abel. – Abel had something to do with it. Maybe he was carrying them or maybe he fell onto them.
> Abel rompió las ventanas. – Abel threw a rock at them or kicked them on purpose.
>
> Se nos olvidó el pastel. – We forgot the cake (but please don't be angry with us).
> Olvidamos el pastel. – This could imply we intended to forget it, which would be rare.
> Olvídalo. – Forget it. (someone telling you to forget about it intentionally)
>
> Se les perdieron las llaves. – They lost their keys and we feel bad for them.
> Perdieron sus llaves. – It may be the same as above, but maybe they lost them in a bet.

¡Ojo! The noun that fell, got broken, forgotten, or lost is the subject of the reflexive verb: *La llave se perdió* or *las llaves se perdieron*. Also, like with most verbs, the subject can be placed before or after the verb: *Se me olvidó el regalo* or *El regalo se me olvidó*. This technique can be done in all tenses and moods.

> *Ej.* No se te olviden los regalos. – Don't forget the presents. (modo imperativo)
> No creo que se te olviden. – I don't think you'll forget them. (subjuntivo del presente)
> Se me ha ocurrido que … – It has occurred to me that … (indicativo, presente perfecto)
> ¿Se os dificulta correr tanto? – Is it difficult for you guys to run so much?
> Se nos hace cada vez más tonto. – It seems/gets more and more stupid to us.

You don't have to be talking about accidents to combine reflexive verbs with indirect objects.

> *Ej.* Se me acercó. – She approached me. (acercarse – to approach)
> Me le acerqué. – I approached her.

Some people may perceive a subtle difference between some verbs and their reflexive form.

> *Ej.* caer – to fall (towards the ground), caerse – to fall (accidentally, like to slip or to trip)
> morir – to die (general), morirse – to die (of natural causes)

Los verbos (el futuro como especulación)

You've seen the simple future tense and its most common use: the future of the present, just like in English (p.67). Another common use of the simple future tense is to speculate or wonder. The phrase "I wonder" could be translated as *me pregunto*, and to say, "I ask myself" would also make sense in English, but that is not the only way to speculate or wonder in Spanish. That's where the simple future tense comes in.

Imagine this scenario: you and your friends are out at the park playing soccer. No one has a wristwatch anymore and no one brought their cellphone to the game. After seemingly hours of playing, one player turns to the other players and says, "I wonder what time it is." The person making that statement is making the assumption that no one knows exactly, but invites the speculation from the group. In Spanish, the simple future tense is used and phrased in the form of a question. If you want to respond with speculation, saying, "I bet," just make it a statement.

> *Ej.* I wonder what time it is.   (Me pregunto) ¿Qué hora será?
> Could it be after 8:00?   (Me pregunto) ¿Serán las ocho pasadas?
> I bet it's around 7:30.   Serán las siete y media.

No one knows for sure, but that doesn't stop anyone from speculating. Certainly, they could say, *"No lo sé, que no tengo reloj conmigo,"* but where is the fun in that?

Imagine another scenario: you and a friend are hanging out at your house, watching a movie late at night. Suddenly, you both hear a knock at the door. You aren't expecting company and it's too late for it to be a political canvasser. You don't ask your friend, *"¿Quién es?"* because you know your friend has less of a clue than you; it's your house, after all. So, naturally, you speculate.

> *Ej.* Who could that be?   (Me pregunto) ¿Quién será?
> Maybe it's the neighbor.   (Me pregunto) ¿Será un vecino?

This speculation works for any verb, not just *ser*.

> *Ej.* I wonder how old they are.   (Me pregunto) ¿Cuántos años tendrán?
> I wonder what's for dinner.   (Me pregunto) ¿Qué habrá de cenar?
> I bet he comes here every day.   Vendrá acá todos los días.

What if you want to speculate about the past? You got it: you use the conditional tense.

> *Ej.* I wonder what she did for a living.   (Me pregunto) ¿A qué se dedicaría?
> I wonder why it was closed.   (Me pregunto) ¿Por qué estaría cerrado?

This works for the future and conditional perfect tenses, too.

> *Ej.* I bet he's sold his car.   Habrá vendido su carro.
> I wonder if he'd already seen it.   (Me pregunto) ¿Lo habría visto ya?

Los verbos (el imperativo) – nosotros y vosotros

By now, you are quite familiar with commands (pp.55-58) and how they compare to and contrast with the indicative and subjunctive moods. You are now ready to learn the last two pieces of the puzzle: *nosotros* and *vosotros*. Whereas the *vosotros* form is a true command, the *nosotros* form is more of a suggestion to a group that includes the speaker (exhortative). The best translation is "Let's ____." That said, *let's* fill in the gaps from a previous chart (p.57).

apoyar

(+) **yo:** ------------   (+) **nosotros:**   apoyemos (basically subjunctive)
(–) **yo:** ------------   (–) **nosotros:** no apoyemos (basically subjunctive)

(+) **tú:**   apoya   (+) **vosotros:**   apoyad (as with *tú*, not simply subjunctive)
(–) **tú:** no apoyes   (–) **vosotros:** no apoyéis (basically subjunctive)

resolver (o → ue)

(+) **yo:** ------------   (+) **nosotros:**   resolvamos (basically subjunctive)
(–) **yo:** ------------   (–) **nosotros:** no resolvamos (basically subjunctive)

(+) **tú:**   resuelve   (+) **vosotros:**   resolved (as with *tú*, not simply subjunctive)
(–) **tú:** no resuelvas   (–) **vosotros:** no resolváis (basically subjunctive)

influir (y)

(+) **yo:** ------------   (+) **nosotros:**   influyamos (basically subjunctive)
(–) **yo:** ------------   (–) **nosotros:** no influyamos (basically subjunctive)

(+) **tú:**   influye   (+) **vosotros:**   influid (as with *tú*, not simply subjunctive)
(–) **tú:** no influyas   (–) **vosotros:** no influyáis (basically subjunctive)

Some argue that the only "true" command forms are *tú* and *vosotros*, affirmative forms, all the rest being simply the subjunctive. While that is a legitimate way to look at it, that argument breaks down with the placement of object pronouns in the affirmative command forms.

imperativo: (nosotros) apoyémoslo   **subjuntivo:** (nosotras) que lo apoyemos
             (vosotros) apoyadlo   (vosotras) que lo apoyéis
             (ustedes)   apóyenlo   (ustedes)   que lo apoyen

imperativo: (nosotros) resolvámosla   **subjuntivo:** (nosotras) que la resolvamos
             (vosotros) resolvedla   (vosotras) que la resolváis
             (ustedes)   resuélvanla   (ustedes)   que la resuelvan

When the pronouns attached to the *nosotros* command form begin with *se* (pp.43, 53), the first *s* is dropped.

             conseguir (e → i) (e → i)   comprar

(+)   consigámoselas (consigamosselas)   (+)   comprémoselo (compremosselo)
(–) no se las consigamos   (–) no se lo compremos

Although the double *s* is not permitted, there is no problem with double *n*, which you encounter when combining *nos* with the *Uds.* command form.

conseguir (e → i) (e → i)   **comprar**

(+)   consíga<u>nnos</u>la   (+)   cómpre<u>nnos</u>los
(−) no <u>nos</u> <u>la</u> consigan   (−) no <u>nos</u> <u>los</u> compren

Similar to the cases of double *s* on the previous page, watch what happens to affirmative commands of reflexive verbs for *nosotros* and *vosotros*: the *s* and *d*, respectively, are dropped.

dormirse (o → ue) (o → u)   **sentarse (e → ie)**

(+)   durmámo<u>nos</u> (durmámo~~s~~<u>nos</u>)   (+)   sentémo<u>nos</u> (sentémo~~s~~nos)
(−) no <u>nos</u> durmamos   (−) no nos sentemos

(+)   dormí<u>os</u> (dormi~~d~~os)   (+)   senta<u>os</u> (senta~~d~~os)
(−) no <u>os</u> durmáis   (−) no <u>os</u> sentéis

There is one exception to the rule above for reflexive verbs in the *vosotros* form: *irse*. Instead of dropping the *d*, the correct affirmative form is *idos*.

You've noticed that the affirmative *vosotros* commands are formed by replacing the *r* of the infinitive with a *d*. *apoyar → apoyad*, *resolver → resolved*, *influir → influid*, etc. The coolest thing about this is that there are no exceptions. *ser → sed*, *ver → ved*, *ir → id*

Remember our list of irregulars whose *yo* forms in the present had a unique conjugation (p.58)? With the affirmative forms of *vosotros* being all regular, and the rest being, with the exception of pronoun placement, the same as the subjunctive, the gaps in our chart are easy to fill in.

salir	(+) vosotros: salid	(−) no salgáis	(+/−) nosotras: salgamos
tener	(+) vosotros: tened	(−) no tengáis	(+/−) nosotras: tengamos
poner	(+) vosotras: poned	(−) no pongáis	(+/−) nosotros: pongamos
traer	(+) vosotras: traed	(−) no traigáis	(+/−) nosotros: traigamos
hacer	(+) vosotras: haced	(−) no hagáis	(+/−) nosotros: hagamos
ver	(+) vosotros: ved	(−) no veáis	(+/−) nosotros: veamos
venir	(+) vosotros: venid	(−) no vengáis	(+/−) nosotros: vengamos
decir	(+) vosotras: decid	(−) no digáis	(+/−) nosotros: digamos
ser	(+) vosotras: sed	(−) no seáis	(+/−) nosotros: seamos
dar	(+) vosotros: dad	(−) no deis	(+/−) nosotras: demos

Although predictable in the *vosotras* forms, the *nosotras* forms of *ir* and *irse* have alternatives.

ir	(+) vosotras: id	(−) no vayáis	(+/−) nosotros: vayamos / vamos
irse	(+) vosotras: idos	(−) no os vayáis	(+/−) nosotros: vayámo<u>nos</u> / vámo<u>nos</u>

With all the dropped letters and exceptions, you see why I separated these two from the rest.

Los verbos (el voseo) – Verbs (the use of *vos*)

Vosotros, used in the Castilian dialect (central and northern Spain), is an alternative to the 2nd person, plural form *ustedes*. Likewise, in many countries, there is an alternative to the 2nd person, singular form *tú*. While not universal, this alternative is called *vos* and is used in at least one region of almost every country in Central and South America. According to the *Real Academia Española*, these countries are Argentina, Bolivia, Chile, Colombia, Costa Rica, Ecuador, El Salvador, Guatemala, Honduras, Nicaragua, Paraguay, Uruguay, and Venezuela.

The conjugations for *vos* are the same as those for *tú*, with the exception of the present tense (indicative and subjunctive) and affirmative commands. Even though Spain uses *vosotros*, but not *vos*, and the countries that use *vos* do not use *vosotros*, their conjugations share morphological origins, as do the words themselves: *vosotros* (*vos* + *otros*).

	vosotros (present / [+] command)		vos (present / [+] command)
caminar	camináis / caminad	→ (drop the *i* and *d*) →	caminás / caminá
comer	coméis / comed	→ (drop the *i* and *d*) →	comés / comé
vivir	vivís / vivid	→ (no change, drop the *d*) →	vivís / viví
pensar	pensáis / pensad	→ (drop the *i* and *d*) →	pensás / pensá
volver	volvéis / volved	→ (drop the *i* and *d*) →	volvés / volvé
pedir	pedís / pedid	→ (no change, drop the *d*) →	pedís / pedí
estar	estáis / estad	→ (drop the *i* and *d*) →	estás / está
dar	dais / dad	→ (drop the *i* and *d*) →	das / da
tener	tenéis / tened	→ (drop the *i* and *d*) →	tenés / tené
poner	ponéis / poned	→ (drop the *i* and *d*) →	ponés / poné
traer	traéis / traed	→ (drop the *i* and *d*) →	traés / traé
hacer	hacéis / haced	→ (drop the *i* and *d*) →	hacés / hacé
ver	veis / ved	→ (drop the *i* and *d*) →	ves / ve
ser	sois / sed	→ (drop the *i* and *d*) →	sos / sé
venir	venís / venid	→ (no change, drop the *d*) →	venís / vení
decir	decís / decid	→ (no change, drop the *d*) →	decís / decí
salir	salís / salid	→ (no change, drop the *d*) →	salís / salí
ir	vais / id	→ (drop the i, change the verb) →	vas / andá (just like *andar*)

¡Ojo! Neither *vosotros* nor *vos* observes stem changes. The written accent marks on the *vos* forms are necessary to maintain the emphasis on the same syllables as those of *vosotros*.

Finally, let's look at reflexive verbs.

sentarse	os sentáis / sentaos	→ (drop the *i* and *d*) →	te sentás / sentate
ponerse	os ponéis / poneos	→ (drop the *i* and *d*) →	te ponés / ponete
vestirse	os vestís / vestíos	→ (no change, drop the *d*) →	te vestís / vestite

Los verbos con preposición

Mastering prepositions in another language is a tall task. Between English and Spanish, you can't simply learn a single translation for each preposition and call it a day unless you want to sound like a foreigner forever. In one context, one translation may work, but in another context, it may betray you. I recommend you learn prepositions in relation to the verbs that require them. As with every list in this guide, this list is not all-inclusive, but it is a good start.

acceder (a)
acostumbrarse (a)
asomarse (a)
atreverse a + *inf.*
animar a + *inf.*
asistir (a)
aprender a + *inf.*
ayudar a + *inf.* – to help to __
comenzar a + *inf.*
conducir (a)
contribuir (a)
dirigirse (a)
dedicarse (a)
decidirse a + *inf.*
echarse a + *inf.*
enseñar a + *inf.*
empezar a + *inf.*
esperar (a) – to wait (to)
enfrentarse (a / con)
faltar (a)
forzar a + *inf.*
ir a + *inf.*
impulsar a + *inf.*
incitar a + *inf.*
limitarse (a)
llegar a + *inf.*
oler (a) – to smell (like)
obligar a + *inf.*
ponerse a + *inf.*
parecerse (a) – to look (like)
prepararse a / para + *inf.*
resignarse (a)
renunciar (a)
recurrir (a)
saber (a) – to taste (like)
sonar (a) – to sound (like)
tender a + *inf.*
mandar a + *inf.*
unirse (a) – to join
volver (a) + *inf.* – to _____ again
abusar (de)
acordarse (de)

acabar de + *inf.* – to have just + *past participle*
alegrarse (de)
apoderarse (de)
aprovecharse (de)
arrepentirse (de)
avergonzarse (de)
asegurarse (de)
burlarse (de)
contagiarse (de)
convencer (de)
cubrir (de) – to cover (in)
cambiar (de)
carecer (de)
cansarse (de)
depender (de) – to depend (on)
disfrutar (de)
divorciarse (de)
darse cuenta (de)
dejar de + *inf.* – to quit/stop _____ing
dudar (de) – to doubt
despedirse (de)
enamorarse (de) – to fall in love (with)
embarazarse (de) – to become pregnant (with)
emocionarse (de)
encargarse (de)
enterarse (de)
hartarse (de)
irse (de)
llenar (de / con)
ocuparse (de)
olvidarse (de)
pensar (de) – to think / have an opinión (about)
preocuparse (de)
quejarse (de)
reírse (de)
separarse (de)
servir (de) – to serve (as)

salir (de)
vestirse (de)
acabar (con)
contar (con) – to count (on)
compartir (con)
comprometerse (con / a) – to commit (to)
comenzar (con / por)
cumplir (con)
casarse (con) – to get married (to)
encontrarse (con)
empezar (con / por)
enojarse (con / de)
llevarse (con)
pelearse (con)
relacionarse (con)
reunirse (con)
soñar (con) – to dream (about / of)
tener que ver (con)
tropezarse (con)
ayudar (en / con) – to help (with)
consistir (en) – to consist (of)
confiar (en)
convertirse (en)
dudar (en) – to hesitate
entrar (en / a)
especializarse (en)
fijarse (en)
frustrarse (con / de)
influir (en / sobre)
interesarse (en)
insistir (en)
involucrarse (en)
meterse (en)
molestarse en + *inf.* – to bother _____ing
pensar (en) – to be thinking (about, in the moment)
sentarse (en / a)
tardar (en)

112

Por vs. para

You've seen examples of *por* and *para* in context, but maybe you've never seen any rules describing their usage. As with *el pretérito/el imperfecto*, *ser/estar/haber*, and *saber/conocer*, the English translation will not help you distinguish *por* from *para*. Both mean "for" in multiple cases. The key is to learn their uses in context. You could substitute with the phrases in parentheses.

- **Use *por* in the following contexts:**

  - in favor of (*a/en favor de*) — (Luchamos *por* la libertad. Votó *por* el demócrata.)
  - in search of (*en busca de*) — (Voy [a] *por* agua. Vinieron [a] *por* mí.)
  - instead of (*en lugar de*) — (Trabajé *por* Joel porque él estaba enfermo.)
  - on someone else's behalf — (Tengo vergüenza *por* él; ¡qué tonto es!)
  - cause or reason (*a causa de*) — (No jugamos *por* el viento. Chilló *por* miedo.)
  - in exchange for (*a cambio de*) — (Pagaron $10 *por* la camisa. Le di eso *por* esto.)
  - duration of time (*durante*) — (Camina *por* 30 minutos. Fue doctor *por* 30 años.)
  - general time frame (*en*) — (Me baño *por* la noche. Tomo café *por* la mañana.)
  - means of transportation (*en*) — (No les gusta viajar *por* autobús. Viajaré *por* tren.)
  - means of communication — (Habla *por* teléfono. Me comunico *por* WhatsApp.)
  - through (*a través de*) — (Anduvimos *por* Cusco. Corrí *por* los pasillos.)
  - along or by (location) — (Juegan *por* el río. El parque queda *por* la librería.)
  - multiplication and division — (5 *por* 5 son 25. 12 dividido *por* 3 son 4.)
  - velocity — (Corrimos 10 millas *por* hora.)
  - frequency (*al/a la, cada*) — (Trabajo 8 horas *por* día. Ganan 30.000 € *por* año.)
  - gratitude — (Gracias *por* tus sugerencias. Gracias *por* todo.)
  - congratulations — (Felicidades *por* tu premio.)
  - apology — (Discúlpame *por* molestarte. Perdón *por* el ruido.)
  - passive voice with *ser* — (El poema fue escrito *por* Octavio Paz.)
  - the future — (Estoy emocionado *por* el concierto este viernes.) (Tengo miedo al huracán que está *por* venir.)

- **Use *para* in the following contexts:**

  - destination or direction (*a, hacia*) — (Nos vamos *para* Puerto Rico. Salió *para* la playa.)
  - intended recipient of something — (El regalo es *para* mi tío. La compré *para* Nohemi.)
  - use or purpose of something — (La cama es *para* dormir. La leche es *para* mi té.)
  - deadline — (Tengo que entregar el reportaje *para* el lunes.)
  - in contrast to a norm or expectation — (Habla mucho *para* una niña de dieciocho meses.)
  - in order to + *inf.* — (Fuimos al parque *para* jugar al fútbol.)

As you can plainly see, there are far more distinct uses for *por* than for *para*, so if you are in doubt, and have to wager a random guess, the odds are on the side of *por*. For some expressions, like *por favor*, it may be a stretch to find its guiding rule. When you say it, are you asking someone to do something "in exchange for" your favor? Perhaps. Is your *favor* the "cause" or the "reason" for someone's action? Maybe. Some expressions are common enough that they are worth memorizing, regardless of the rule you might apply to it. Memorizing the following idiomatic expressions will help you use *por* and *para* correctly.

- **Idiomatic expressions using** *por*

por lo general – in general / generally
por lo menos (al menos) – at least
por supuesto – of course
por (de) casualidad – by chance
por un lado (por una parte) – on the one hand
por otro lado (por otra parte) – on the other hand
palabra por palabra – word for word
por primera vez – for the first time
por último – lastly
por fin – finally
por ahora – for now
por ejemplo – for example
por ningún lado – nowhere
por todas partes (por todos lados) – everywhere
la razón por (la que/cual) – the reason for (which)
por accidente – by accident
seguido por (seguido de) – followed by
por (de) nada – it was nothing / you're welcome

por separado/a – separately
por cierto (a propósito) – by the way
por eso – for that / that's why
por lo tanto – therefore
por consiguiente – consequently
por ende – thus
por desgracia – unfortunately
por suerte – luckily / fortunately
por si acaso – (just) in case
por favor – please
por ciento / por cien – percent
por adelantado – in advance
por completo – completely
por el amor de dios – for the love of god
¡Ay, por dios! – Good lord!
por medio de – by way of
por lo visto – apparently
por poco – barely / narrowly / just

- **Subtleties between** *por* **and** *para*

¿por qué? – why? / because of what?
¿para qué? – in order to what? for what purpose?

por arriba – (from) (up) above
para arriba (hacia arriba) – upward

por fuera (afuera) – (on the) outside
para afuera (hacia afuera) – (to the) outside

por abajo – (from) underneath / down below
para abajo (hacia abajo) – downward

por dentro (adentro) – (on the) inside
para adentro (hacia adentro) – (to the) inside

por aquí – this way / over here
para acá – over here / in this direction

para siempre – forever (more common)
por siempre – forever (less common)

por allí – that way / over there
para allá – over there / in that direction

hay muchas cosas para hacer – there are a lot of things to do
hay muchas cosas por hacer – there are a lot of things that remain to be done
hay muchas cosas que hacer (hay que hacer muchas cosas) – … a lot of things that have to be done

- **Idiomatic expressions using** *para*

para colmo – to top it all off
ser elegible para – to be eligible for
para más información – for more información
cambio para un billete de $20 – change for a $20 bill
tener problemas para + *inf.* – to have problems (with) _____ing

aplicar para (solicitar) – to apply for
cualificar / calificar para – to qualify for

El español mal hablado

In graduate school, I took a course on discourse analysis. We had a guest professor one day who asked the class, "*¿Qué es el español?*" One by one, we shouted out completely valid answers, but none of them was what he was looking for. Finally, we relented, and he indulged us. "*El español,*" he said, "*es el latín mal hablado.*" Throughout my bachelor's and master's programs, there wasn't a single utterance more impactful on the way I approached the Spanish language—or language in general—than that one. Language is living, ever changing, pitting each generation against all previous ones.

In 1492, Spanish was officially declared a language as the regional kingdoms were unified into one single Spanish kingdom. For centuries prior, there was the educated class, which spoke Latin, and the uneducated class, which spoke a progressively more bastardized form of Latin (street Latin, if you will). This street Latin, no longer intelligible by citizens of other countries that supposedly also spoke Latin, was, by virtue of its unintelligibility, a new language. Thus, *Español*—or *Castellano*, as it is known in some Spanish-speaking countries—was born. From *El cantar del mío Cid* to *El ingenioso hidalgo don Quixote de la Mancha* to the Spanish taught in schools across the globe today, the Spanish language has evolved and will continue to evolve until it is no longer spoken by anyone on the planet.

One of the stated goals of the *Real Academia Española* is the preservation of the Spanish language. While this is commendable, it is inherently a losing fight. The reality is that even the prestigious *RAE* is aware that the Spanish language is evolving, and they continually update their dictionaries to reflect modern linguistic trends. In the same discourse analysis class I mentioned earlier, we went on to discuss "prescriptive" vs. "descriptive" grammar. Prescriptive grammar is that which attempts to teach people the correct way to speak (write, etc.), whereas descriptive grammar attempts to identify and document the way people speak. Both are completely valid points of view. The more fluidly you can move from one to the other, the better communicator you'll be.

If the point of language is to communicate, then the most effective form of communication is to speak the other person's language, literally and figuratively. Sometimes asking "How are things, my brother?" will resonate with someone on a deeply human level, and other times it will draw laughs and mockery. In contrast, "Sup, brah?" may make the connection you are looking for, and other times it may get you uninvited to the next academic conference.

If you are like me, your curiosity is insatiable and you want to know every detail of the Spanish language. I encourage you to indulge that passion, keeping in mind that not everyone shares our passion for detail and that there are factors beyond the academic side of language that play into effective communication. I've had to learn to relax and go with the flow when I hear native Spanish speakers make grammatical errors. Even when my interest is just to understand why they chose to say what they said, I've had to bite my tongue for the sake of the interaction. If you are talking to your college professor or your local Spanish tutor, ask away. If you are talking to a client or trying to navigate your way through a foreign country, take it in stride and focus on the connection with the person in front of you, not on their word choices. If you are not like me, and you don't get caught up in the "why" of everything, well, then, disregard this paragraph.

My last lesson to you—given what you know about my take on the Spanish language—is obviously tongue-in-cheek: "*El español mal hablado.*" Every language has its idiosyncrasies and oddities; some people label them as errors and some label them as regionalisms. The beauty of it all is that you get to decide how you interpret them.

- ***"Laísmo," "loísmo," and "leísmo"***

Laísmo and *loísmo* are the improper use of direct-object pronouns (*lo, la, los, las*) in place of indirect objects.

    Ej. "La di un beso" (Le di un beso)   "No la dije nada" (No le dije nada)

Un beso is the direct object since it is the "what" you gave. That means what is missing is the "to whom" you gave the *beso*. This is the indirect object that should be represented by the pronoun *le*. *Nada* is the direct object, therefore the person should be the indirect object (*le*).

Leísmo is the improper use of indirect-object pronouns (*le, les*) in place of direct objects.

    Ej. "Le vi ayer" – "*le*" representing a woman (La vi ayer)

The "what" you saw is the woman, and although it is a person, not an inanimate object, it still is the direct object.

These linguistic phenomena can be found in regional pockets all over the Spanish-speaking world. One interesting oddity is that in Spain, *le* substitutes for *lo* only when referring to a human direct object (masculine, singular). Although not universal, it is academically accepted.

    Ej. le abracé (a mi tío)   los abracé (a mis tíos)
          la abracé (a mi tía)   las abracé (a mis tías)

Although "*lo abracé*" (*a mi tío*) is academically accepted and prevalent in Latin America, it sounds odd to many Spaniards, as though "*mi tío*" were being treated as less than human.

The *Real Academia Española* (www.rae.es) has a *Diccionario panhispánico de dudas* (drop-down menu from their home page), which tackles the trickiest, most highly debated topics in the Spanish language. If you search "*leísmo*," you will find everything you could want to know on the matter. The *RAE* is both prescriptive and descriptive in its approach, telling you the academically accepted norms without shying away from giving examples in literature that deviate from the recommended usage. Search individual verbs if you're not sure if they need a direct or indirect-object pronoun.

    Ej. servir*le* or servir*la*? molestar*le* or molestar*la*? llamar*le* o llamar*la*? etc.

Regardless of what the *RAE* recommends, for every expert in one country who says "*ayudarle*" is a clear example of *leísmo*, there is another expert in another country who says "*ayudarla*" is a clear example of *laísmo*. Perhaps the best advice I ever heard regarding this dilemma was from a Colombian classmate of mine in graduate school: "*a cada quien, según su propia realidad.*"

- **Borrowed words**

Spanish, like every other language, has incorporated many words borrowed from English. Some are exactly as they look in English: *jeans, hockey, parking, mall, hall,* etc. Some require a little brainwork to decipher: *guachimán* (watchman), *barman* (bartender), *living* (living room), etc.

116

- **Mispronunciations, malapropisms, and other linguistic oddities**

Surely you are guilty of at least one of the following mispronunciations in English, most likely without knowing it:

Ej. "ignowledge" (acknowledge), "spinage" (spinach), "ostridge" (ostrich), "perserverance" (perseverance), "fermiliar" (familiar), "expecially" (especially), "expresso" (espresso), "pundant" (pundit), "infinant" (infinite), "architectual" (architectural), "jewlery" (jewelry), "nucular" (nuclear), "acrost" (across), etc.

Do you know other people who mispronounce these words? Do you cringe when you hear them or do you take it in stride? Do you judge them? What about when people use the wrong word (malapropism) or butcher an idiomatic expression or erroneously and unintentionally mash up words? We all do it from time to time. Sometimes it leads to laughter and sometimes we coin a new word that we later can't imagine not having at our disposal, like "brunch" or "webinar."

Ej. lay (laid, have laid) vs. lie (lay, have lain), accept vs. except, "lip sing" (lip sync), hunger "pains" (pangs), "tow the line" (toe the line), "for all intensive purposes" (for all intents and purposes), "I could care less" (I couldn't care less), "it begs the question" (it raises the question), "refudiate" (repudiate + refute), etc.

There is a psycholinguistic basis for these "misspeaks." Sometimes we misapply or over apply a rule. Sometimes we don't understand the origin of a phrase, so we make up what we think the person must've ("must of") said. This is often subconscious, and I'm sure there are quite a few psycholinguistic studies on the matter. The following are common errors you'll hear from native Spanish speakers from time to time. Don't let them rattle your faith in what you've learned, but feel free to embrace them as cultural oddities without passing judgment. I would also encourage you not to adopt them for yourself, as the more standard your Spanish is, the more universally understood and accepted your communication will be.

Ej. "muncho" (mucho), "haiga" (haya – confused with *haga*?), "fuistes, hablastes, comistes," etc. (fuiste, hablaste, comiste, etc. – over applying the "*s*" associated with the *tú* form), "dijieron, trajieron," etc. (dijeron, trajeron, etc. – misapplying the regular ending -*ieron*), "nadien" (nadie – supposed plural form?), "habían dos carros" (había dos carros – treating the direct object as the subject of *haber*, which doesn't exist), "siéntensen" (siéntense – over applying the "*n*" associated with the *Uds.* form), "detrás mío" (detrás de mí – treating the adverb *detrás* as a noun), "cercas" (cerca), "a voz de pronto" (a bote pronto – not understanding the origin of the phrase), etc.

Sometimes *a* gets erroneously attached to another word due to its prevalence in other structures.

Ej. "qué agusto" (qué gusto – <u>a</u> mi gusto, estoy <u>a</u> gusto, etc.)
"quiere averte" (quiere verte – <u>a</u> ver, vamos <u>a</u> ver, etc.)

Sometimes irregular verbs are taken as regular verbs.

Ej. tostar (o → ue) "tosta" (tuesta), degollar (o → üe) "degolla" (degüella), plegar (e → ie) "plega" (pliega), cocer (o → ue) "coce" (cuece)

Some errors are very consistent, some deliberate for ease of pronunciation, and others for reasons that are beyond my powers of perception and intuition.

> *Ej.* *e → i*: "voltiar" (voltear), "airopuerto" (aeropuerto), "pior" (peor), etc.
> *s → j* before *k* sound: "ej que" (es que), "ejcuela" (escuela), "ejquina" (esquina), etc.
> *f → j*: "juimos" (fuimos), "jueron" (fueron), "jumar" (fumar), etc.
> *ue → uo*: "fuogo" (fuego), "juogo" (juego), "luogo" (luego), "puodo" (puedo), etc.
> the dropping of *ll*: "tortía" (tortilla), "cae" (calle), "se ama" (se llama), etc.
> the dropping of *d* in words ending in *ado*: "lao" (lado), "pescao" (pescado), etc.

If American English is your first language, you'd probably understand, "I am going to the store," if you heard someone say, "Ama go the store." Why ask, "do you want to?" when you can say, "wanna?" Perhaps you're from Scotland or New Zealand and can teach me a thing or two about *your* colloquial English that I wouldn't otherwise understand. Think about non-native English speakers; what do you think their chances are of understanding the meaning when they hear this kind of nonsense? Slim to none, and Slim just left town, as my dad would say. It's not that it's spoken too quickly, it's that it isn't spoken clearly. As you travel the Spanish-speaking world, you're going to have to adapt to how others speak because, chances are, they won't adapt to you. So, when you hear a Mexican ask, "*¿Quihúbole?*" or a Colombian exclaim, "*¡Hijue!*" or a Chilean ask, "*¿Comestái?*" etc., cut yourself some slack. In every country, you'll find some people who speak clearly and some who decidedly do not. Just do your best and forget the rest.

- **Americanisms and other regionalisms**

There are probably more than a dozen ways to say *bueno* in Spanish when you not only consider different eras, but also every tiny pocket and corner of the Spanish-speaking world. How many can you name in English? Cool, neat, sweet, fresh, rad, bad, legit, dope, righteous, boss, sick, wicked, def, gnarly, dank, bitchin, tight, hip, groovy, tubular, wizard, etc.

> *Ej.* chévere, chido, suave, padre, genial, a todo dar, buena onda, guay, bacán, chulo, etc.

If you want to say you like something, don't limit yourself to *me gusta* and *me encanta* when you can throw out a Mexican "*me late*" or a Spanish "*me (súper) mola.*"

Why say, *sí* in the U.S. when you could say, "*simón*" or *no* when you could say, "*chale*"?

Don't let the name *Real Academia Española* fool you; it's not just for Spain. Check out their *Diccionario de americanismos*: http://lema.rae.es/damer. Here you'll find words that their *Diccionario de la lengua española* does not have registered.

> *Ej.* monitorear, troca, agendar, etc. (don't let anyone tell you these are not words)

It also has *calcos*, which are words that already had one or more meanings in Spanish, but because of their similarities to foreign words or some other foreign influence, they've taken on new meanings colloquially.

> *Ej.* carpeta – file folder (now carpet), ratón – mouse (now mouse for a computer), etc.

Some common words or phrases in one country sound silly in another and may not be understood or even accepted. So, if you learn a phrase in one country, or from this guide, then a native Spanish speaker says that's not how you say it and tries to correct you, don't let it shake your faith in what you know to be true; simply ask them how they would say it and add it to your repertoire.

> *Ej.* When fruit goes bad, you'll hear "*se echó a perder*" in Mexico, but in Spain, they say, "*se estropeó.*" Each sounds ridiculous to the other culture. If you say "*según yo,*" in Mexico, you won't raise an eyebrow; if you say it in Spain, brace for laughter.

Some words or phrases have different meanings in different countries, leading to frequent miscommunications between native Spanish speakers.

> *Ej.* In many countries, *chillar* means "to scream," wheareas in others, it means "to cry." In some countries, *qué pena* means "how sad," in others, "how embarrassing."

Some words or phrases have a normal, everyday meaning in some countries, but in others, they are vulgar and offensive. I don't mean to be vulgar or offensive here, just informative, so you don't get yourself into trouble.

> *Ej. Fregar* means "to scrub" or "to wash," but in some countries, it means "to screw over." *Coger* means "to grab" or "to take," but in some countries, it means "to f**k."

So, when a Spaniard tells a Mexican that she is going to *coger un taxi*, it's met with either laughter or indignation. In the Caribbean, *la guagua* means "the bus" and they *cogen la guagua* all the time. In some countries in South America, *la guagua* means "the baby." You see how easily you could get into trouble!! A similar case in English is the word "bugger." In the U.S., it describes children when they are naughty, and you might even hear a little old lady say it as an exclamation. Outside of the U.S. (and maybe Canada), it absolutely does not mean a naughty child!

- **Euphemisms, double meanings, and innuendos**

Like English, Spanish has its euphemisms (*ay chihuahua, no manches, caray, joroba, ostras,* etc.), as well as double meanings and sexual innuendos. These also vary by country/culture.

> *Ej. hacerse una chaqueta, hacerse una paja, correrse la paja,* and *volar la cometa* can all mean *masturbarse. Echar un polvo,* among countless other phrases, means *tener sexo.*

Some foods in Spanish are euphemisms for genitals, like "nuts," "weiners," and "clams" in English. This will explain the chuckles you get when you say them completely innocently.

> *Ej. la panocha* (type of pastry), *el chocho* (little candy or pastry), *la papaya* (papaya), etc. *la salchicha* (hot dog or sausage), *el plátano* (banana), *el chile* (chile pepper), etc.

- **Espanglish y code switching**

"Espanglish" is a mashup of words like "*cheeseburguesa*" and "*no me toches.*" Code switching *es cuando personas* alternate between *idiomas durante* the same conversation. *A veces*, it's because they don't know certain words *en los dos idiomas*, and sometimes *se hace porque* one language captures a sentiment *mejor que el otro.* To language purists, *es una aberración, pero para algunos*, it's part of their culturo-linguistic heritage y *se expresan mejor así. Curioso*, isn't it?

Apuntes

Apuntes

About the Author

David Faulkner holds bachelor's and master's degrees in Spanish, with an emphasis in teaching, and has taught Spanish in every grade from fourth to the university level. He is passionate about the fundamentals of language, as well as interpersonal communication and personal expression, particularly where their practical application has a positive impact on people's lives.

Faulkner opened up about his childhood in his memoir, *Superheroes* (2015), and has since shifted his focus back to his true calling: teaching Spanish and inspiring others to practice it in their daily lives.

Faulkner enjoys spending time with his family, public speaking, traveling the world, and staying active. He is an idealist and a relentless dreamer, reveling in the happiness of pursuit. *De cabo a rabo* (*Gramática*, *Vocabulario*, and *Actividades*) comprises his second, third, and fourth books.

To schedule David Faulkner for a curriculum presentation to see how his Spanish guides could benefit your language program, or to hire him for private lessons or as a guest teacher at your school, please contact him through DavidFaulknerBooks.com.

Flashforward
Publishing

Made in the USA
Middletown, DE
10 August 2020